Post-Traumatic Growth

A Story of Injury and Recovery

Jesse Hewitt

Post-Traumatic Growth
A Fortis Vult Publishing Book
All Rights Reserved
Copyright © 2024 Jesse Hewitt
Editing by Jessie Anderson
Formatting by Damian Jackson
Cover Art by Andre Costa Vianna

No part of this book may be reproduced or transmitted, downloaded, distributed, reverse engineered, or stored in or introduced into any information storage and retrieval system, in any form or by any means, including photocopying and recording, whether electronic or mechanical, now known or hereinafter invented without permission in writing from the author.

Hardcover Book ISBN: 978-1-7780408-5-6
Paperback Book ISBN: 978-1-7780408-7-0
Electronic Book ISBN: 978-1-7780408-4-9

To my wife Jessie, whom is the sole reason I wrote this book and who's support has been instrumental in my recovery. I love you.

To my children Keaton and Ellie who I adore. Your sense of adventure and enthusiasm keep me young and exhausted. I love you both.

Special Note

Please see the trigger warnings contained within each chapter prior to reading the personal anecdote.

Difficult themes are discussed.

Personal anecdotes are provided which may be upsetting to some readers as their contents can be descriptive and may articulate details or discuss events which can provoke distressing, emotional reactions.

Passages containing personal examples are in *italics* – please skip these passages if you are not comfortable reading their contents. We understand.

Please read with care.

Resources and contacts for Mental Health Supports

1. *The Suicide Crisis Helpline* is available by dialing 988
2. *Boots on the Ground* is a help line for first responders by first responders. Phone number: 1-833-677-2668.
3. *Crisis Centre Chat* is a website that allows you to talk online to someone for mental health.
They also have extra numbers for mental health support and online services for adults and youth.
Website: https://crisiscentrechat.ca/
4. *Text Hotline for Mental Health, Depression, and Anxiety* is available 24/7. Text: 686868 and talk via text.

If you, or someone you know is struggling, please contact a Mental Health Care or Medical Professional to seek further support.

Contents

Foreword	ix
Introduction	xi
1. Emotional Wounds	1
2. Hypervigilance	9
3. Flashbacks & Understanding Dissociation	19
4. Exposure Therapy	25
5. Anxiety & Panic Attacks	41
6. Managing Intrusive Thoughts of Homicidal Ideation	50
7. The Right Professional for You	59
8. Lack of Support in the Workplace	65
9. A New Perspective on Old Ways	71
10. Muscle Memory & Physical Health	88
11. Equine Therapy	96
12. Post-Traumatic Growth	104
References	115

Foreword

In 2020 I went in to see a psychologist, for what I thought, would be a routine assessment. I walked out of that appointment having been diagnosed with the following: *PTSD with Dissociative Symptoms, Major Depressive Disorder with Recurrent Episode – severe – with Suicidal and Homicidal Ideation, Alcohol Use Disorder and Bulimia Nervosa – Moderate to Severe.*

I was *floored.*

I had left the army three years earlier, in 2017, after serving twelve years, with an honorable release to pursue a career in a municipal police service. I figured that by leaving the army, I would have left those symptoms behind me as well. Man, was I wrong. Ignoring the issues and symptoms only made them grow stronger. They began encompassing my life to a point where it crumbled around me, ending my new career and my reputation. Not only that, it's been a constant burden in the family court proceedings of the custody access of my two children. At my worst in 2016, I would stare at my service pistol on the table at home and drink, contemplating ending the pain. I was a broken man, and I blamed the world around me for years after I was first injured in 2014. The injury was difficult to talk about at the time, because it was purely psychological. I was self-destructive and blamed

Foreword

everyone but myself. I ended up nearly homeless and spent time living in a trailer park for months. I needed help, desperately, and after swallowing my pride and listening to my friends and family I dedicated my effort into improving my mental health. After years of talking, support and rehabilitation, I am pleased with my progress and able to report that I'm recovered. I decided to write this book so those who have suffered like me know that they're not alone. I want them to know that it's okay to get hurt, it's okay to suffer, and it's okay to ask for help. Don't believe that you're suffering alone and don't believe that it can't get better. I'm proof that it can, and now that I can stand again, I'm ready to support those who can't. If this book can be a crutch to help someone, anyone, steady themselves and to get help and begin recovering, then the objective was met.

I'm not the man I was before getting hurt. I'm better.

Introduction

Stop me if you've heard this one before: a broken marriage, resulting with a single mom raising two young boys in a low-income home. Hamburger Helper for dinner several times a week, with at least one step-father figure that was abusive emotionally and physically, either to the mother, the children, or to all parties.

Typically, those scenarios result in one of two outcomes. Once the kids are raised, they either become small-time criminals or trades workers in blue-collar jobs with little to no education. That's the stereotype, and I believe they exist for a reason. I very nearly fell into both of those categories myself at various points in my life. Every other weekend growing up, I would spend a couple of days with my father. He only has an education to the level of Grade 10; he has an easy-going attitude and the only work he's ever known has been that of a bricklayer. My father spent what time he had with me teaching me what he knew of stonework and giving me and my brother more freedom and leeway than any child should have from the ages of 6-8. It was a normal weekend for us if we had either BB guns or .22 rifles and spent our time walking around the back-forty, picking off porcupines in trees or walking a couple kilometers to the river to fish with dug up

Introduction

earthworms. In hindsight it was a phenomenal childhood, one rarely seen outside of movies. That lack of supervision would get me into trouble, and it taught me lessons that helped prepare me for a future as both a solider and a police officer. My parents are polar opposites. The trouble would begin at my father's and the responsibility for the consequences of those actions would fall upon my mother once my brother and I had been returned, sometimes in one piece, sometimes not.

At 11 years old, I was dragged to the local police station by my mother after having a BB gun war with other kids my age. We shot out every window of a parked school bus at a farm during the summer break. After the damage was done, we -decided the next best thing was to shoot at each other, obviously! I was shooting blindly over the seats and I smoked one of my friends in the cheek with a BB. It went through one cheek and into the other in the side of his face. We trudged the walk of shame back home, and myself, my brother, and our three friends gave the same story, "It was an accident!". The explanation we gave to all of our parents failed to mention that we destroyed an entire school bus a single county over.

Well, two weeks later, my childhood conscience couldn't handle the guilt of it any longer. I caved and told my mom the night before school. As a single, working mother of two boys, I'm sure you can imagine the hell that she was prepared to unleash upon us. I expected a thrashing, verbal and perhaps even physical, which would educate me as much as Homer's *Iliad* or the *Odyssey* would years later. Smart woman she is however, she knew what would really impact me.

She went to bed that night telling me she would deal with my brother and I in the morning. I knew that the worst was coming. I'm the older brother by two and a half years and I was the one that shot the bullet which shredded my friends face, turning him into a childhood Joker I found out that morning, after lying to my mom about the whole incident for two weeks. The kid actually *had* gone to the hospital to have the BB removed from inside his face. Not my proudest moment, even as a troubled kid.

The next morning after breakfast, my mom told my brother and I

Introduction

that we were going for a drive. I expected to be driven to school – we lived so far in the country that we had to take two different school busses to get there. To get to school however, you needed to turn left at the end of the dirt road we lived on. My mother did not turn left. In fact, she turned right, and at that point I knew it was over for me, though I didn't know how the end would look. Thirty minutes later I was in a local police detachment and left in the Sergeants office with my brother – my mother simply drove away. The two of us were read the riot act by the most massively intimidating, yet also soft-spoken, man I had met at that point in my young life. I couldn't look that man in the face; I was so embarrassed and ashamed of what I had done. I sat there for about forty-five minutes being calmly spoken to about what could happen to me regarding charges for the damage I had caused to both the property and the injury to my friend's face. He also explained to me that the owners of the bus, and my friend's parents, could sue me and my family for damages as well as, now, he was required to phone them to explain what he had learned of the incident. I sat across from him in a chair beside my brother, my head hanging so low that I couldn't tell if my brother was crying like I was, or if he had the balls to look the Sergeant in the face. He did not.

After the calmest verbal "lashing" I had ever received was over, I told the Sergeant I understood, all the while not being able to look him in the eyes. He escorted us outside where I saw my mother had returned and was waiting for us in the car. I was furious. I blamed her for everything, even though I knew it was my fault. I hated her and I didn't speak with her for at least a day or two; an eternity for a kid living with a single parent.

It took a long time for me to mature and realize that what my mom did by dropping me off at the police station was in my best interests. I learned a lesson about myself that didn't sink in for several years – that sometimes I need to sit and avoid having a narrow-minded perspective or one-track mind. It put me in a position to hate the ones who were working in my best interests, and I refused to recognize their position or how weak my frame of mind was.

Introduction

I recognize now, years after suffering from mental trauma, that in that moment, I stubbornly refused to acknowledge the perspective of others trying to help me on several occasions. I fell into depression and it was easier to hide the symptoms by burning myself out at work, partying, and playing video games. That lack of self-awareness – which is also a part of dissociation, which I'll explore my experience with later – prevented me from being able to properly begin the healing process. The foundation for recovery was not established psychologically for me, and in the end, it resulted in me blindly hating myself, my loved ones, and those who were trying to help me, by acting like an angry child who had been tricked into taking responsibility for his criminal actions.

I grew up in the country, which meant a lot of bush parties in the back-forty and drinking too much. Actually, "too much" meant a twelve pack of Coors Light would have put me and one of my friends in the ditch hammered; being teenagers none of us had the stomach to drink much more than that without being sick. I earned extra keep, and incentives (like a free trip to a concert) by doing jobs for my neighbours, one of which was splitting wood after football practice for six weeks to get tickets to see Ozzy Osbourne, and gas for a ride to the concert. Life could have been much harder, and I would learn while serving overseas a decade later, just how hard other people had it.

I joined the Army Reserves in high school as an infantryman, doing my basic training, soldier qualification and infantry qualifications over the summer months when I wasn't in school. I went from a fat, 5'8 teenager of over 230lbs, to a nearly sickly thin 145lbs after "battle-school". Eating rations and living in the woods, doing nothing but mock attacks on an enemy position, carrying a 75lb machine gun and doing reconnaissance (recce's) on 'enemy' positions all day and night for months got rid of the excess weight I was carrying in my body. Those months taught me a lot about mental fortitude and humbled me while helping to prepare me for life going forward.

I ended up finishing high school and moving five hours away from home to go to Niagara College. Upon graduation, I moved to the neighbouring Brock University. I met my ex-wife while at university and,

Introduction

after I was done, I joined the army again – this time as a member of the military police (I am now happily remarried). After the six-month course to become qualified as a military police officer, I was posted to my first position in Ottawa, where I would spend a couple years as a patrolman. I loved being a military police officer (MP), but the workload wasn't great and I needed to keep busy. I felt that I wasn't being challenged enough so I started looking into applying to the special forces. I felt that I could contribute more than what I was currently accomplishing in my role as an MP. I was going to apply to the Canadian Special Operations Regiment (CSOR), but I ended up being talked into applying to the Close Protection specialty within the Military Police by a colleague. Applications were only open to members of the infantry or military police. To apply you needed to meet a minimum physical standard of fitness when you submitted your application.

Upon submission, if your application was competitive enough, you'd be selected for the 'CPAC', otherwise known as the Close Protection Assessment Course. I was flown from Ottawa to British Columbia for a week to engage in the most physically demanding week of my life. I lost nearly 15lbs, and when I got home my spine was compressed from the weight I was compelled to lug around. I was almost two inches shorter, and it took three weeks to get back to normal. To this day, that has been the only experience where I could actually *feel* pain in my bones! There were eighty candidates that applied to go to CPAC, forty of which were selected for that phase of the selection process in BC. The selection process was broken down into phases that assessed each candidate's physicality, mental fortitude, and attitude. Additionally, there was a comprehensive psychological assessment. Of those forty people, eighteen either finished but were unsuccessful passing the board's psychological assessment, or they passed the board's evaluation. The board is a collection of assessors and psychologists that evaluated each candidate's performance and capabilities and this aspect of the course is held at the end of the process. Of the selected eighteen candidates which were found suitable for the CPOC, Close Protection Operator Course, I was lucky enough to be one of them.

Introduction

The candidates, most of whom I still talk to eight years after the course, drove from Canada to North Carolina, USA. We worked out of what was formerly known as Blackwater, XE, Academi, or whichever name it decided to take that particular year. To this day, it is one of my favorite experiences throughout my training career. We had the opportunity to train in environments that simulated what several of us would deploy to just a few months after the two-month course finished. In my opinion, the facilities available to us in that environment surpassed anything I've ever seen in Canada. The level of expertise provided by both the American and Canadian staff was outstanding and helped prepare me for what happened both domestically and internationally as I participated in operations as part of a Close Protection Team.

After successfully graduating with fifteen other candidates at the end of Summer 2012, I returned to Ottawa to resume my role as a Military Police patrolman for several more months. I was not tremendously impacted by any calls as an MP psychologically. Although, I can't speak for many of my peers. I have friends whose quality of mental health has suffered as a result of careers where the mental and physical burdens placed upon them, either by a single event or experiencing consistent negative stimuli throughout their career, was extremely impactful. People suffering from a mental wound from a single traumatic event are at as much risk as an individual who has suffered repeated exposure to negative stimuli, to experience ongoing symptoms as a result of the trauma. I have several friends who have been traumatized by overexposure to negative stimuli while working child sex offender investigations. Their trauma was not physical, but the repeated exposure to horrible pictures and videos that they were required to sift through in order to get evidence to convict monsters had a long-lasting negative impact on them.

Looking back on my childhood, I can't help but feel grateful for the lessons that I learned and those imparted to me by others. A lack of leadership as a child led me down a potentially dark path, but my mother and loved ones were able to intervene and ensure I learned consequences through tough love. Those experiences shaped me into becoming the man I am today. Every misstep, accomplishment, crime,

Introduction

and good deed I'd ever committed played a role in the development of my character and my resilience to injury, both physical and psychological. No person is infallible, as I can attest, and no person is invincible to the experiences life will throw at us. Trauma, whether physical or emotional, impacts us and can change us forever. Untreated trauma however, damages us further and can lead to us losing ourselves.

Chapter 1
Emotional Wounds

When I'm asked about scenarios that I've lived through, those which resulted in a diagnosis of PTSD, I find that some people expect to hear a war story that holds nothing back; something akin to a Hollywood movie. In reality, it's never a heroic situation that's reflected upon fondly, and the experience very well did not result in a happy ending. The psychological trauma resulting from the multiple psychological injuries is something I live with daily. Instead of breaking down the situation to a stranger, reliving it in my mind as I speak the words, I choose to tell people that inquire that I'm not comfortable with talking about the negative stimuli that resulted in my injury. I find it's an easier and more articulate way of expressing that a horrible incident occurred, without going into detail that could flare up the symptoms I live with. I know what happened to me, and sometimes (most of the time), I don't feel the need to explain every event in detail which affected me years prior. This book is the exception in some cases. It's not that I'm afraid to talk about those incidents, though I used to be. The reason is that I've told people who were not military, police, or first responders, some of the stories and they are utterly horrified. I feel like their horror is directed at me as a person, as though, somehow, *I'm* the monster rather than the people responsible for what happened. After experiences like that, I've chosen to simply say 'negative stimulus' rather than explain the particulars of any situation I went through, unless I'm speaking to a counsellor or doctor conducting an assessment or helping me with rehabilitation.

In my experience, and by no means am I an expert, I've found that many of the PTSD symptoms have a delayed onset, sometimes only surfacing months, or even years, after first experiencing the trauma which is the root of the psychological injury. After returning home from my last deployment, I was given a pamphlet with a list of symptoms to watch out for, as this was a general rule of thumb from the army for returning soldiers. It was recommended that three months after returning, soldiers go see a social worker or psychologist to talk about any issues that may have arisen since being home.

The issue is putting the onus on the individual to be watchful for mental health issues in themselves, rather than having external supports appointed to assist in watching for signs of struggle. How on earth is someone who is suffering from delayed onset PTSD, burnout, or any slew of other mental health issues, capable of conducting that level of self-reflection? I would suggest that, often, they can't…. just as I couldn't. I didn't see how my injuries were reflecting upon me and changing me as a person. I was becoming less and less of the person I was and I was changing into something else entirely. I couldn't consciously identify that I was suffering from psychological injuries and instead I began "self-medicating" (which is a nice way of saying I hid away from my troubles with booze). I didn't even know I was drinking more alcohol than normal at first. It took some intervention by friends and family who told me that they were concerned I had been drinking too regularly and, at first, I was in complete denial. I refused to acknowledge that I had begun drinking to excess nearly every night of the week, let alone see that I was suffering in other areas of my life as well. I had blinders on. By stubbornly refusing to accept the concern others were trying to provide me, I was setting myself up to die.

I didn't realize at the time, but I was bleeding out psychologically. I needed to stem the flow, but first I needed to find out where I was bleeding from.

Post-Traumatic Growth

Where was the injury?

What was the injury?

It isn't as simple as tying a tourniquet above a severed limb or cut artery. I was bleeding out from trauma coming from my psyche, and I needed to figure out a way to stop it immediately.

There are several differences and similarities between physical and psychological trauma. A physical wound will cause pain, and the longer it bleeds, the less blood there is flowing to your brain. As your life's blood is leaving your body the pain lessens as you become more exhausted. The initial adrenaline rush that helped you finish that gunfight, make that arrest, or finish that fight, for example, is gone and now you're realizing how bad of a spot you're in. If you don't stop the bleeding, you're going to pass out from blood loss and die. Those last moments before bleeding out are confusing and tiring. People suffering from surprise lethal physical trauma generally don't want to die.

That's the main difference between severe physical and severe emotional trauma. When the emotional or psychological trauma is *that* severe, the feelings of pain and exhaustion never recede. If anything, the symptoms grow worse and worse without easing up. Eventually there is no facete of your life where you're not in pain. It gets to a point where the psychological trauma is so great that you feel like you can't go on any longer. Those feelings can manifest into conscious self-loathing, depression, feelings of inadequacy, etc. In my case, the psychological trauma was so significant that I contemplated ending it in the only concrete way I knew how – by killing myself. Thankfully, I received help and nothing happened that could not be reversed and recovered from. Frankly, I find it easier to deal with physical trauma over mental health. It's also easily visible, eliminating those thoughts of "am I really injured?", as you can clearly see that the injury when it's manifested physically. Thoughts of doubt regarding my mental health quality and whether or not I was truly suffering plagued me for years, feeding my urge to resist finding help.

Let me elaborate.

Jesse Hewitt

Personal Anecdote
Trigger Warning – Discussion of Suicide

My most significant emotional downfall was a night in my home, in my basement, in 2016. I had been burned out from work in the army for a while, and I hadn't yet sought out a mental health professional to help address the undiagnosed injuries I was unaware I possessed. I knew I was having a hard time at work, but I lacked the ability to reflect on my own mental health and determine that I was having significant issues with depression and alcohol abuse. Work was a mile-a-minute position and I never stopped moving. I would come home from work at night with my service pistol on my hip. We wore civilian clothes at the unit I was attached to in the military. A badge that we hung on our belts displayed our military profession to the public to ensure they knew we weren't gun-toting maniacs in collared shirts and khaki pants.

I was deeply depressed at this point, but still undiagnosed, and I couldn't find happiness or enjoyment in anything anymore. I was constantly in and out of the country on short deployments, or in the USA working at their facilities to help train soldiers as part of the Close Protection Operator course, or assisting with Pre-Deployment Training to deploy to Afghanistan and Iraq.

The days were long and I would come home at night and drink and play video games online with the same peers I had worked beside all day. I couldn't shut off my brain from work, and it's all I really cared about. My problems magnified however, when I gradually became more disillusioned with my career, finding reasons to hate it or hate myself. I was numb emotionally, and whenever I was on a tasking overseas, I would hope for a bomb to go off so I could finally just die. The longer I worked, the more the pain and depression I was feeling sunk deeper into my bones and became a part of me. I was barely sleeping due to nightmares. I hadn't gone to see a social worker or counsellor yet, and I was consciously refusing to acknowledge that I was having issues. Instead, I was blaming it on everything going on around me at home and at work.

The pain was so deeply set into my mind and body that I was

Post-Traumatic Growth

walking around feeling like a corpse every day of the week. The drinking helped numb some of the symptoms. The rest I avoided by tuning myself out of reality and playing video games. Through the booze and the games, I was attempting to escape from the painful reality I was living in at the time.

One night however, I went down to the basement with a six-pack of beer that I had picked up on my way home. I took my gun off my hip and laid it on the rec room table and sat on the couch.

That night was different though, and I didn't turn on my TV.

I just sat there and drank in silence, in the dark, and stared at my pistol the entire time. I thought to myself how easy it would be to end the pain and exhaustion I felt every single day without any foreseeable end. I sat like this until all the beers were empty, feeling emotionally numb the entire time.

The feeling of contemplating suicide isn't as it's portrayed in movies, at least it wasn't for me. I was emotionally distant and calculating. I made a mental list of the pros and cons of it, and the cons greatly exceeded the pros. I decided that I simply couldn't hurt my family like that, and I had too much responsibility and people who depended on me.

It wasn't an emotional decision for me because, at that time, I had suppressed all my emotions and felt nothing anymore. I decided not to kill myself based on the responsibilities I had at the time. As simple as I made the decision to keep living, I remember shrugging my shoulders when I stood up, unloading my gun and throwing those empty beer bottles out.

It was shortly after that night when I had my first bad anxiety attack which prompted me to finally see a counsellor.

About 30% of first responders have PTSD, and veterans are two times more likely to commit suicide than civilians (Abbot et al., 2015). Suicidal Ideation is reported amongst first responders, including EMS/paramedics. The research available now shows that, not only do first responders who typically attend to conflictual scenarios, such as police officers and members of the military, but first responders who attend to any emergency situation/trauma, including fire-fighters and EMS, experience the same suicidal ideation (Abbot et al., 2015).

One study reported that 37% of both fire-fighters and EMS have contemplated suicide, which is 10 times the number of American adults (Abbot et al., 2015). More specifically, a breakdown of fire-fighters in the USA regarding suicidal ideation, plans and attempts, were rated at 47%, 19% and 15.5% respectively (Stanley et. Al., 2015).

Another study showed that fire-fighters were reported to heavy or binge drink approximately 50% of the time, and that 50% of fire-fighter deaths are attributed to stress and/or exhaustion (Haddock et. Al., 2017). The same study reported that 40% of female fire-fighters self-reported binge drinking in the last month, with 4.3% of them admitting to driving while intoxicated. This leads to the assumption that these self-destructive behaviours are not gender-oriented, and that psychological injuries affect both men and women within first-responder roles.

There can be pre-existing conditions that may make some people more at risk than others for certain psychological injuries. Some of these include poor physical conditioning, unfit mental health due to either exterior or pre-existing trauma, and those who have suffered from physical injuries. These conditions can lower the mental resilience available to these individual first responders.

Resilience, otherwise known as the ability to handle and adapt to exterior stress while maintaining psychological prowess, is what protects us from the injury. Just as some people are natural athletes compared to the rest of their peers, levels of resilience can be naturally higher in some people and lower in others. Life experiences, both positive and negative, effect the level of resilience in a person, but it can also be grown and improved through training. The more prepared a mind is to experience trauma, the less likely that trauma is going to break through the resiliency barrier and create a psychological injury resulting in depression and other PTSD symptoms. Every day a person's resilience is tested. Poor sleeping quality due to injuries, chronic pain, and obesity all diminish a person's resiliency and puts them more at risk of illnesses such as depression and anxiety (VanDen-Kerkof et. Al., 2011).

Training resiliency needs to occur prior to an event that would require resiliency to protect the individual, immediately post-event, and periodically in the extended time afterwards for first responders (EMS, Fire-fighters, Police, Military to name a few). Social support amongst peers, ensuring good relationships exist with the individual and his or her leadership, and a healthy home life, are all key to ensuring the wall of resiliency is stable and strong. The realities of the jobs that have high-stress, and where people frequently encounter traumatic events, need to be made clear. Frank and candid discussions post-event need to be encouraged and *must* occur.

It is also crucial to understand that the families of first responders (and other high-stress careers including deep sea welders, oilfield workers, etc.) are sponges for the stress post-event once those members have come home. They are not typically granted training opportunities to ensure their resilience levels are strong and capable. Psychological injuries within the family dynamic are possible should the family not be prepared for the amount of post-event stress and trauma that the member brings home with them. Frankly, there is a reason the divorce rate amongst first responders (fire, EMS, police, soldiers, etc.) is higher than other civilians, and I attribute that to the level of stress that first responders and their families are exposed to every day as it bleeds into the personal lives of these men and women.

We all have a responsibility to take care of ourselves and our families, and to watch over our peers when exposed to trauma. It's okay to be hurt. It's not okay to ignore the injury and let it fester. The research available shows that first responders have a high rate of suicidal ideation in relation to trauma experienced on the job. Pre-existing conditions such as poor physical health, pre-existing trauma and physical injuries make first responders more vulnerable to psychological injuries.

Resilience, or the ability to handle and adapt to stress, can protect against these injuries, but it can also be improved through training and conditioning. The mental preparation assists in preparing these members for the post-event stress that they bring home after a traumatic incident. It's everyone's responsibility to take care of themselves and their families and be aware of the impact of trauma on first responders and their families.

Chapter 2
Hypervigilance

In 2014, I was part of a Close Protection unit assigned to protect embassy staff in Tripoli, Libya. This was only a couple years after the beginning of the 'Arab Spring' in 2011, which had led to the overthrow of several Middle Eastern dictators, including the Ghaddafi dictatorship which had been in power for over forty years.

This was also two years after the infamous 2012 Benghazi attack against a USA compound, leading to the deaths of USA Ambassador Chris Stevens, United States Foreign Service (USFS) officer Sean Smith, and Central Intelligence Agency (CIA) contractors Tyron Woods and Glen Doherty.

Even people born and raised after the 9/11 attacks have learned about the global impact and how it impacted the change in security and policy within the United States. Soldiers from the USA and Canada are still stationed in Middle Eastern countries that originated a decade earlier as the response to the attacks on September 2001.

The overthrow of the Ghadaffi government and his dictatorship led to Ghadaffi's capture and subsequent torture, followed by his death. The extrajudicial killings did not stop with the end of Ghadaffi's government however, they proceeded to extended through his son Mutassim, who was captured as his father had been. Additionally, nearly one hundred other loyalists to the Ghadaffi regime that were captured that day were rounded up near a local hotel and shot dead. The fervor of the Libyan people was so intense that it bubbled and boiled in the political atmosphere in the years after the celebration of their dead dictator. That boiling point came to a climax in 2014, with the end result being total civil war within the country and the evacuation of every embassy in Libya. It was unexpected and I suffered significant psychological injuries as a result of several incidents (or negative stimuli) that I was exposed to during this mission, in several incidents over the course of the five-month operation until we evacuated the Canadian Embassy and its personnel.

The team and the embassy personnel lived in the area west of Tripoli, on the northern coastline called Janzur. The sea north of us was the Mediterranean, with Naples, Rome and Sicily being on the other side of the sea. The countryside was beautiful, with thousand-year-old monuments from the Roman Empire still standing in the city. We operated in civilian clothes, drove armored SUVs, and carried concealed small arms (pistols), while keeping carbines and other tools in the vehicles. That eventually changed as the threat level transformed in the area, requiring a more overt (heavily armed) presence from us. We kept carbines in the vehicle with bug-out bags, (bags packed with ammo and essentials to grab and get out of that area as quickly as possible) ready for when/if shit hit the fan and we needed to evacuate at a moment's notice.

We lived on the economy in Libya, meaning that we went out and shopped at local shops for groceries and cooked for ourselves. We had to buy any necessities including water, food, clothing, fuel, and other supplies unless they were readily available through friendly embassies nearby. It was a thirty-minute drive from our living quarters to the embassy building (an office within one of the few completed towers in Tripoli). We had conducted route recognizance (recce's) each morning prior to moving any diplomatic personnel or ambassadors. A minimum of two vehicles was required as escort for a maximum of two diplomats in the lead vehicle. We kept team members within the embassy throughout the day to add additional security, with a desk for the members facing the front door and carbines readied to mow down any intruders who decided to storm the embassy.

The road conditions in Libya prior to the civil war were sufficient for the trips across Tripoli, both to and from, the living quarters to the embassy across the city. We had four 'main' recce'd routes that we would take and randomize each day. One route used the only semi-completed paved highway in the city, a second was paved but was a single lane road, and the third and fourth were dirt roads. The concept of 'routine kills' was heavily implemented as part of our training prior to deployment. The concept is the notion that doing the same maneuver day after day becomes predictable and therefore an easy target to plan an attack on, hence: "Routine Kills". That training put emphasis on avoiding applying the same maneuvers consecutively or repeatedly in a manner that could be predictable to hostile people. Otherwise, if we followed a routine set of maneuvers that could be easily scheduled, it would allow any enemy surveillance to coordinate an ambush, attempt a kidnap, plant ground implanted improvised explosive device (IED) or plant vehicle born improvised explosive device (VBIED).

Vigilance, trained reactions to specific situations and foresight were, and remain, what keeps soldiers and cops alive (as well as any other high-stress, dangerous career). I used the training provided to me while on that operation. Books such as Dave Grossman's *On Combat* teach things such as 'The Warrior's Mindset', which is about overcoming challenge and adversity through physical and psychological leverage (Grossman, 2008). Books and training to ensure that the mind is always present in a fight or conflict situation, helps train a person's body to react a certain way in a fight or flight situation. The training I received both as a soldier and a police officer involve constant situational awareness, scanning for threats and planning ahead for 'what-if' scenarios.

Another psychological tool given to us through training, which I saw used both as a soldier and police officer, was the OODA loop. The OODA loop stands for 'Observe, Orient, Decide, Act', and was developed by a United States Air Force fighter pilot John Boyd. The entirety of the model as a tool is that it trains individuals that mental agility (quick thinking) can overcome raw power (strength in numbers or physicality) when dealing with other people.

The OODA loop is a mental process that is cyclical in nature and constantly in motion. It is meant to be in order to be continuous and instinctive throughout combat. By design, I would observe my surroundings, orient myself to my object, decide upon the best course of action to gain advantage over that objective, and then act upon that decision. The moment that act is completed, the OODA loop resets and is prepared to engage in the next challenge.

The OODA loop is something that every human does unconsciously, without consciously understanding that we're calculating and observing, orienting, achieving and adapting to goals and overcoming obstacles. That method has been utilized to help hone the skills of soldiers, police officers, professional athletes and has even been implemented as part of business models to overcome adversaries faster than they can adapt. This "combat-oriented" training enables soldiers to use the tools at their disposal in order to gain a tactical and lethal advantage over an adversary.

Not everyone's OODA loop is the same. In my observations, I found that natural athletes have a much faster and more developed OODA loop, and I have found that natural athletes use the OODA loop method much more quickly than a non-athlete. Men and women who have competed in competitive sports have a naturally faster OODA loop due to the competitive nature of the sport itself and the training involved to be successful at the competitive level. Most sports are a game of "mental chess" which include a large physical component. Players are in a constant battle with their opponents. Participants try to outmaneuver their adversaries both physically and mentally, as well as engage in a mental battle with themselves with determination and the will to prevail. Seeing the end goal in your mind allows you to plan the path you will follow in the match, competition or battle you are dealing with.

In combat, the OODA loop, tactical chess, or whichever name you choose to call it, has the potential for an outcome that could be lethal to those performing the acts. The objective in a combat situation is to

Post-Traumatic Growth

eliminate the threat. If that threat is a person who has a warrior's determination which mirrors your own, and they refuse to surrender themselves to your aggression, it is very much a lethal battle of wills and determination. Of the two combatants in this situation, the one who possesses a faster performance of the OODA loop will prevail. It is important to remember that, in that situation, it is possible to interrupt the opponent's OODA loop with negative stimulus of your own. The option to overwhelm their senses with aggression, or using tools such as flash grenades, as well as any other number of physical tools is available to both soldiers. Using any of these options puts one at a tactical advantage to increase their chances of winning the fight. First Responders also have a number of choices and resources available to them when faced with a high-intensity conflict scenario.

Now, as a soldier, police officer, fire-fighter, paramedic, or other first responder, it's amazing to have all of these psychological tools to add to your mental toolbox. Tools such as the ability to empathize with others in the middle of an incident, or to hold a commanding presence in order to become the leader at an emergency. Each of these are skills that are passive in nature but provide the ability to control the environment around the person utilizing them. These skills help control the fight or flight response a person has when overwhelmed in an emergency.

The problem is that when you suffer from a mental injury such as depression, PTSD, suicidal/homicidal ideation, an eating disorder or addiction issues, you feel as if you're *always* in a fight or flight scenario, and the skills utilized prior become very difficult to manage. You feel as if, in an instant, you could be in a fight for your life and you find yourself operating at this level of heightened awareness when at home, the grocery store or taking your kids to school. Subconsciously, you are expecting to come under attack from an enemy. At least, that's how it felt for me!

What I'm describing is hypervigilance. I believe it's a normal byproduct of dangerous professions. Being hypervigilant in a warzone keeps you alive. The perpetual scanning of perceived and possible dangers in the area keeps you from missing an exposed culvert, drain pipe or sewer grate when driving through Iraq or Afghanistan. It'll keep your eyes sharp and you'll detect when someone has a bulge behind their back or in their waistline, or how they reach their hand into a baggy coat pocket attempting to access a gun. This level of vigilance is appropriate in very specific instances and allows for appropriate action to prevent a situation from escalating. Hypervigilance becomes a problem when a person cannot shut it off. It becomes a crippling issue when combined with other psychological disorders which originate from negative stimulus. My own experience is one such as this – hypervigilance manifested into something that impacted me every day.

After returning from Libya in the fall of 2014, following the evacuation of the embassy, I was given a small pamphlet that had a list of symptoms to look out for with regards to my mental health and left for home with the leaflet in-hand from Germany. I had my commanding officer and a sergeant waiting for me at the airport to welcome me back at the airport in Canada. I went to my house and had the next month off as part of post-deployment leave. I spent the time learning how to relax and focused on regaining weight as I had lost thirty-five pounds overseas due to the food shortage caused by the civil war. My meals in the last weeks were cans of tuna and stale bread.

After my month of leave I returned to work full-time. I returned to the Close Protection Unit and within four days of being back at work another deployment opportunity arose. The Close Protection Team protecting the Canadian ambassador in Kabul, Afghanistan needed to supplement their numbers. I volunteered instantly, flying out within hours that same day after being accepted for the operation. I didn't realize it at the time, but I was craving the adrenaline dump of going back overseas as soon as I could; I yearned for the exposure of extreme stimulus. I would learn later that the adrenaline rush and seeking out conflict and wanting to be in warzones was part of the injury and aggravating my mental health struggles, but at the time it was addictive. I now understand extreme sports fanatics; people often described as 'adrenaline junkies'.

I spent several weeks assisting with that operation before flying

Post-Traumatic Growth

back to Canada. The flight back was delayed due to a suicide bomber attacking the Kabul airport. My first working day back in Canada was October 22nd, 2014. That was the day Parliament Hill was attacked by a lone gunman in Ottawa, Ontario. The Close Protection Unit and I deployed immediately in armored cars, equipped with carbines and still in civilian clothing (we rarely worked in uniform). By the time we arrived at Parliament Hill, the gunman was dead inside – shot dead by the RCMP. However, there were fears that there were multiple attackers and the possibility that IEDs were in the wood-line slightly north of Parliament Hill. We secured the head of the Canadian Forces, Chief of Defense Staff General Tom Lawson at the National Defense Headquarters. I was then tasked with taking him to Prime Minister Justin Trudeau's residence for an emergency meeting, where the RCMP were also present guarding the exterior of the building in the event of further attacks. After everything was said and done, it turned out that the lone gunman was a mentally unhealthy murderer, who had gunned down Corporal Nathan Cirilo by shooting him in the back with a hunting rifle as Corporal Nathan Cirillo guarded the Tomb of the Unknown Soldier on October 22nd, 2014. It was a cowardly act, and the murderer then ran through the front doors of Parliament Hill, gunned down by police inside after he wounded two others.

Within three months I had been involved in the evacuation of a Canadian Embassy isolated in the middle of a civil war, given a four-hour notice to get on a plan for an operation in Afghanistan and when I returned, I was immediately involved in a domestic terrorist act against our nation's capital. After a little over a week, I was sent to Hamilton, Ontario to recce the area where Corporal Cirillo's funeral would be held. We were so low on manpower at the unit from being tasked so heavily in operations internationally, and domestically, that my Sergeant Major had to drive me to Hamilton so I could sleep. Once I hit the ground, I had to conduct a recce of the area prior to being the driver for the General Lawson and the Close Protection Operator coming in via plane to Hamilton the next day. Once he arrived with his bodyguard, I was their 'limo driver' due to my knowledge of the area.

Jesse Hewitt

There was never enough manpower to do any job that needed to be done, and it quickly added up on each member of the unit.

The workload was so intense that no soldier at that unit had a moment of downtime. I didn't know it at the time, but in hindsight I recognize that my hypervigilance was breaking me down, both mentally and physically. I was becoming a harder man at the cost of becoming brittle, meaning that I was becoming a ticking time bomb. I found myself working harder and harder, and the smallest things would set me off. I was constantly 'at work', even when I was at home. I was constantly seeking out threats or planning for dangerous scenarios. I was exhausted daily but I couldn't sleep. I was devoting more and more of myself to the job, not thinking about the long-term consequences or the effects it was having on me. The hypervigilance that had me on high alert every moment of every day was negatively impacting other aspects of my mental health. I believe that the mental exhaustion of hypervigilance eliminated my ability to handle the other PTSD symptoms I was experiencing, but I hadn't yet consciously acknowledged they were there. I couldn't go to hockey games, enjoy a movie at the theatre, or even go out to dinner without feeling exhausted. I realized later that hypervigilance was a symptom of the PTSD itself, and caused me to have anxiety attacks.

I felt that something was wrong but I didn't consciously acknowledge it. It wasn't until the combination of other symptoms I was experiencing in 2016 culminated, and I forced myself to see a civilian social worker. The worker was contracted by the government to work with soldiers at the local military hospital. She was in her mid-50s, had short grey hair, and had a thin frame. She had a small office but never sat behind the desk when we spoke. Rather, she always sat in a chair with nothing separating the two of us. I was hesitant to talk to her about anything initially, and I was closed off and curt with her. She spoke candidly and I quickly realized that she had an extreme level of experience dealing with soldiers. She could talk to them as easily as I talked to people I had served with overseas. She neither minimized nor 'hero-worshipped' anything I said, and she never asked the stereotypical question, "how does that make you feel?".

Post-Traumatic Growth

I spoke of the symptoms I was feeling at the time, and I learned I was experiencing hypervigilance and other issues (at this time I was still undiagnosed with anything). I told her I was hesitant to be prescribed any medication because I had seen the negative side effects in some of my peers. I told her that if push came to shove however, I would take anything she prescribed me, but that I wanted to exhaust all other options for help first.

One of the several things she explained to me was breathing techniques. Initially, it was the instruction to do long slow breaths each night before bed. It was like meditating for ten minutes, alone before bed, without any other stimulus. I took the time to focus on being still and taking slow, deep breaths. I found myself getting impatient or thinking the whole idea was a waste of time at first. A step I took was to set an alarm outside of the room that I could hear. I made sure I didn't leave the room until I heard the alarm, focusing entirely on just breathing and trying to empty my mind for the entirety of the time I spent in the room. I did this for weeks and I found that, just like hitting the gym for the first time, results were not immediate. Discipline is key and by doing this every night I started noticing that I was beginning to be able to calm down, a little at a time. Practicing breathing techniques, combined with other self-mindfulness techniques I was taught, such as finding a quiet space to close my eyes and focus on emptying my mind and focusing on breathing, all helped me begin to find a semblance of calm.

An aspect of hypervigilance was that I was constantly scanning for threats and preparing for the worst outcome possible in any given situation. I was asked during the counselling meetings how many times I had actually perceived and stopped a threat; versus how many times I surveyed my surroundings and not found a threat. I came up short the majority of the time, unable to give concrete examples of how my hypervigilance had benefitted me in my regular day-to-day. It was infuriating to be in that position. I felt like I couldn't help what I was doing and I knew I needed help. The hypervigilance was a small part of a much bigger problem with my mental health, but I needed to chip away at as much as I could to get healthier. The hypervigilance was a small part of an amalgamation of negative symptoms I was experiencing. They melded together and became convoluted to a point where I couldn't determine what was causing which symptom or how to eliminate those negative behaviors and thoughts. I was getting angry with being questioned, and at that point in my life, when I got angry it would boil inside of me for the whole day and I wouldn't be able to calm down. I would look for an excuse to lash out and attack others around me - it wasn't healthy.

I knew I needed help after taking the time to consider my lifestyle, as well as my thoughts and feelings, and by talking to the social worker I had taken my first real steps to recovery. It was necessary to take a hard look at the symptoms I was feeling, including the hypervigilance. These actions, while they may have helped protect me in dangerous environments and situations, had culminated to negative emotions, thoughts and self-destructive behavior. I needed to practice introspection in order to identify the symptoms that were harming my mental health and affecting my life, my career, and my family.

Chapter 3
Flashbacks & Understanding Dissociation
Trigger Warning – Brutality, Death of Child

I mentioned earlier that on my tour in Libya we had four different routes we would choose from to recce each day. Our choice would depend on threat circumstances provided by our Canadian Intelligence operators, as well as recce's completed by the advance team. Civil unrest, militia strife, kidnappings, traffic and other information was constantly coming in which helped us determine the best possible route to travel with the diplomatic staff and Canadian Ambassador. We needed to be mindful and aware of every choice as the route we would take would be used to transport the diplomatic staff throughout the day. We would recce each of the four routes several times a day, noting any changes to the roads, in the public, potential issues that arose such as broken-down cars or possible VBIEDS, riots or anything else which could pose a threat. One of the routes had a round-about on it. There were two females in all-black burkas who would stand at the outer sides of the round-about most weekdays, begging for a couple Dinar (the official Libyan currency).

As the infighting and power struggles between the rival militias within the country grew, one of the first indications that Ansar al-Sharia was beginning to assert its dominance in the region was the change in the native populace. Women no longer walked around uncov-

ered, where they were commonly seen in hijab *(face covering)* rather than burka *(most conservative covering nearly entire body)*. The men began to wear white thoub more often *(the white robes of a man practicing Islam)*. The shift into more conservative religious practice gave us a heads up that a dominant regional extremist group was moving into the area. We saw the flags identifying Ansar al-Sharia *(meaning "Partisans of Islamic Law")* beginning to fly inside the conservative parts of the city (National Counterterrorism Center (NCTC)) 2023). This group wants nothing more than to establish extreme conservative religious laws *(Westerners refer to this as "Sharia Law")* and to eliminate USA/Western influence from Libya. With Canadians in the country looking as pale as a loaf of bread, you can see why seeing these flags did not make me optimistic about the near future of our presence in the country.

When we saw the women in black burkas, I was not immediately surprised, as ultra-conservative Ansar Al-sharia had made their presence known near and inside Tripoli. These women – or what I presumed were women – were standing on the outer edges of traffic roundabouts hoping for charity from passing vehicles. I assumed that they could have been doing recognizance of the timings of our movements at the time, but I also simply felt bad for them. The infighting had gotten particularly nasty within the city by July 2014, with local militia's fighting against one another constantly, even fighting without halting during Ramadan except for prayer. The militias in Tripoli were as loyal to money as they were to ideology. There was a universal hatred for any Ghaddafi loyalists and memorabilia, and the constant power struggle for territory and influence kept the militias at odds with one another. There were nearly a dozen militias of sufficient size to hold territory in and around Tripoli. One would control the airport, while another controlled a hospital, and another still would control a section of major roadway. Each of the militias were heavily armed with spoils from the regime overthrow only a few years earlier, including tanks, heavy machine guns, explosive ordnance, and even gold-plated AK-47's. I once saw a militia post a guard at a gas station armed with a single grenade that he would juggle in front of horrified customers.

Post-Traumatic Growth

At night they would angle their technicals (the name of pickup trucks with 50 caliber machine guns mounted in the bed of the truck), and fire hundreds of rounds in the sky on an angle as a show of force to other rival militias in the area. The problem was that those bullets went up, and they eventually had to come down. We heard "through the grapevine" of intelligence that hundreds of people were dying from raining bullets shot by the half a dozen militias which were vying for control of their regions of the city to maintain control of their territory. You can imagine my heartbreak when on one of the days I was driving through the city and, at that same roundabout, one of the women I'd seen regularly was cradling the body of a small boy in her arms. The boy looked to be about six years old. The boy was wearing a dirty shirt and shorts, with socked feet. He was limp in her arms, and very thin. He was dead. I couldn't determine what caused his death with the visual I had.

I felt sympathy for these women, and I assumed that the child was a relative, possibly even one of their sons. We could not stop to talk to them or offer any help due to the threat level in the area. Our priority was the safety of the diplomatic staff inside the vehicle. Several months into the mission, several friendly nations (which was every embassy within Tripoli), had experienced their staff members getting kidnapped including a Jordanian Ambassador, a USA soldier, and others. I began looking at the women with additional scrutiny as I saw them more frequently over the passing days, seeing them each time I was near the traffic roundabouts conducting recognizance for the safety of Canadian diplomats. The weather was very hot at this time of the year. It was in the summer and the Libyan desert has been recorded to have over 50 degrees Celsius (122 degrees Fahrenheit) temperatures – a heat so hot that the face of my watched cracked. As the days rolled into the second week of them being seen regularly, the women continued to beg for money when the days were cool, or in early mornings and evenings, typically before dusk. The child's body was succumbing to the heat of the environment, degrading and unnaturally sagging in certain areas of his body – clearly, he was beginning to rot.

It was a horrifying and disgusting thing to behold. I witnessed it daily. I was helpless to offer any aid. In the middle of the second week of the 'women' attending the traffic circle I noticed something strange that I had missed before when not paying particularly close attention to the two females. I noticed now that the women had changed in size. They wore black burkas but were clearly not the same two women that had been cradling the body of the child originally. We had a night move (recognizance) one night in the second week of the mission and, as I was driving through the roundabout, I saw a lump near an overpass beside the roundabout. I recognized the lump as the body of the child.

I realized that evening, to my disgust and horror, that several groups of people were using the found body of a child to try and gain sympathy and money from passing drivers. Once the body's utility to gain sympathy was done at the end of the day, the body of this child was discarded like trash, picked at by scavengers until it was rendered useless.

There were no operating police services, fire response teams, nor paramedics or ambulances available in the country at the time. There was no one to pick up that child, return him to his family and properly bury him. That child died and his corpse was treated with such disregard, neglect and disrespect, that I cannot think of someone I hate more to this day than the people who used his body for a couple dollars, only to then toss the body aside like garbage. That body would have been torn apart by scavenging dogs and cats in the area until nothing was left, and I doubt anyone knew what his name was, nor did they care.

Post-Traumatic Growth

That situation has caused me grief over the years because, had I known the child's body was being used as a pawn at the beginning when I first saw them, I feel as though I could have done something. I still feel that the people responsible for doing this should be dead. I felt so much anger in the years after I got home, that I wished I could have executed them on the side of that roundabout. I suffered what would later be diagnosed as dissociation, and I believe this situation is one of the causes for that.

I was officially diagnosed with PTSD with dissociative symptoms in February 2020. I had been experiencing the symptoms of it for years prior to the diagnosis. As is the nature of the injury, with regards to veterans, suffering for a significant period of time before the diagnosis is, in fact, the norm. I had no idea what 'dissociative symptoms' were when I saw it on the report I was given. I needed to ask my doctor for an explanation in order to understand.

Dissociation is a disconnection between a person's thoughts, feelings, memories, behaviours, and perception. It can include emotional numbing as well as sensory, somatic (physical), affective (emotions), and cognitive reexperiencing (reliving past traumatic events within the mind,); including amnesia or other gaps in awareness and memory. Dissociation is linked heavily with PTSD, and studies have shown that those suffering from PTSD currently had higher dissociation scores than those who had either recovered from PTSD or never had it to begin with (Dorahy and Van der Hart (2014)).

A significant number of studies have been done showing the connection between PTSD and dissociation. In a review of 13 studies assessing dissociation on PTSD and trauma-exposed non-PTSD samples, it was found that 11 of the 13 studies demonstrated higher rates of dissociation in the PTSD group. The presence and severity are higher in those who have PTSD compared to those who have non-trauma-related conditions (Dorahy and Van der Hart (2014)). During an assessment of survivors, 12 months after a traumatic event, assessors found that of the 17 PTSD symptoms, only the dissociative symptoms of flashback and amnesia differentiated those with PTSD from those with other psychiatric disorder.

Jesse Hewitt

My interpretation of that study is this: flashbacks and amnesia in relation to PTSD are common and normal symptoms to suffer from. It shows me that men and women who suffer from flashbacks, amnesia and the numerous series of other symptoms associated with PTSD, are not 'weak' for suffering. The National Institute of Mental Health states that 60% of men and 50% of women experience flashbacks after a traumatic event (2021). Flashbacks are an extremely common symptom for someone who is suffering from extreme trauma, and by no means does it make you less of a person or less capable because you're coping with a psychological injury.

For the layman such as myself, I learned to recognize that dissociative symptoms were known in a more personal sense as flashbacks, emotional numbing, amnesia and through physical symptoms such as rapid heart rate, sweating, trembling, tightness of chest, muscle tension to name several. Dissociation is not simply a mental health condition; it has effects on your body as well. Those reading this may understand the physical effects of dissociation through instances of hearing voices, feeling alien in your own body, experiencing physical emptiness or pain in areas that suffered injuries during intense nightmares or flashbacks, etc.

I was able to address and heal from the flashbacks, but it took having to take a long look at myself and admit to existence of the psychological injuries I was suffering from.

Chapter 4
Exposure Therapy

I found that I did not realize the depth of the psychological injury/injuries I had sustained until I was experiencing dissociative symptoms years after the initial occurrence(s). The difference between a physical injury and a psychological one is that the physical injury is typically recognized immediately due both the physical pain and the visibility of the damage, whereas a psychological injury can go undetected. In my case, psychological injuries became known to me only after I had experienced reminders of the incident in the form of flashbacks and other forms of dissociation. If I experience a trigger, to this day, I am open to experiencing various responses as a result of the psychological injuries I am living with.

Jesse Hewitt

Personal Anecdote
Trigger Warning – Witnessing Death

One such psychological incident occurred during the Operation L.O.B.E. in Tripoli, Libya in 2014. Once the civil war had begun, even the citizens caught in the middle of the fighting wanted to escape. There were generally two recognizable ethnicities in Libya. There were those who looked 'Middle-Eastern' in skin tone – meaning tanned skin - and those who were of very dark skin, as seen in countries such as Mali, south of Libya. The dark-skinned Libyans were slaves, no question. They were in a subclass of society that possessed no visible rights within the country. In the mornings you would see them sitting underneath an overpass wearing nothing but a pair of trousers or a loincloth. Barefoot, their skin would be a nearly ghostly white because of the amount of dust coating them. In their hands was a single working tool, usually an old wooden hammer, or maybe a chisel. These men (I never saw a single dark-skinned female in the time that I was in Libya) would jump in the bed of a pickup truck that a light-skinned Libyan would drive. These men were never permitted to ride in the front seats of a vehicle driven by a light-skinned Libyan. On one occasion I saw a goat in the passenger seat while the men sat in the pickup truck bed, revealing exactly where the dark-skinned Libyans fell on the social hierarchy.

When the civil war was on the doorstep of Tripoli, civilians were fleeing the area in whatever way they could. Fleeing east was not an option, as the invading militia forces and Ansar al-Sharia were travelling from the east to the westward side of the country, razing monuments and cutting the heads off opponents, as well as non-Muslims, along the way. Migrating south was not an option for most civilians either, due to the Libyan desert and they were forced to flee to some of the poorest nations in Africa (Niger and Chad for example). With one of the hottest deserts on earth south of the city, and enemies approaching from the east, there left only two options: escaping to the west or escaping to the north.

Fleeing west required a vehicle and enough fuel for a twenty-hour

Post-Traumatic Growth

drive. Fleeing citizens would need to take into consideration checkpoints set up by militias, possibilities of armed robbery/hijacking, and having a passport to show at the border crossing into Tunisia. Those were massive obstacles for many people, including those who were a part of the diplomatic mission we were attached to. The cheapest, and most available option for many of the light-skinned and dark-skinned Libyans, were to get a boat in order to sail north towards Rome or Greece. Unfortunately, that led to the deaths of many civilians.

I saw the aftermath of the attempted escapes on several occasions. We lived in an area that bordered on the sea and my back window showed the beach, which was about fifty meters away. There were days when the bodies of men and women would wash up on shore, victims of capsized boats that were not big enough to survive the waves at sea. These people had hoped to become refugees in safer countries to the north, and died trying to flee war. I would wake up some mornings and watch as the bodies washed ashore, and without any ambulatory, fire department or other emergencies services in existence since the Ghadaffi regime overthrow, the corpses of these people laid there until someone took the initiative to remove them from the beach. Scavenger animals like dogs and cats were common in Libya, and, if the bodies were not removed, they would inevitably go through the process of rotting and being pulled apart.

I never once swam in the Mediterranean Sea after seeing that happen. I returned home from tour and avoided large bodies of water. I didn't go swimming again until after 2017. I had to consciously make an effort to acknowledge and disclose my extreme discomfort around water to a social worker. The sight of it reminded me of the bodies washing ashore and I didn't like the thought of being helpless and unable to do anything for those people who were just trying to flee war. I felt like we could have done more for those people instead of watching civilians be injured and killed as collateral damage in a tribal civil war over a broken country.

I worked through my discomfort with open bodies of water by talking about it with a social worker and beginning exposure therapy. This was largely self-guided at first. Given the nature of the trigger, I could easily remove myself from that stimulus if it became overwhelming. Severe injuries, like a concussion and an operational stress injury (OSI) become easier to obtain with repeated injury. This means that one injury of this nature can make an individual susceptible to reinjury without prudent caution; self-preparation is a constant practice. It's extremely important to keep in the back of your mind that just because the symptoms of the injury have receded, it doesn't mean that it's permanently gone. I think of these as Post-Traumatic Stress Injuries – I try to avoid the use of the term Post-Traumatic Stress Disorder (PTSD) because the term 'disorder' is associated with very negative connotations. You'll see me reference them as injuries several times going forward. I relate these akin to injuring a tendon that requires physiotherapy to heal and recover. Like any other ligament injury, a little physical therapy and hot/cold compresses go a long way. However, just because the pain is gone momentarily, it doesn't mean that you should stop doing physiotherapy, or stop stretching or using those hot/cold measures to massage your injuries. Jumping back into the activity which caused the injury in the first place will only set you back further in the long run. The injury will become aggravated and prevent you from attaining the level of performance you were at prior to straining that tendon. Mental injuries are similar in this manner, and it's critically important that you maintain what I refer to as 'mental physiotherapy' practices. You can notice small improvements when participating in whatever therapy is working for you, but just because you've noticed small positive changes, it doesn't mean you should consider yourself healthy and ready to get back at life thinking the past is behind you. The necessity to 'stick it out' and maintain both life's momentum, and getting that professional help, is critically important. I haven't suffered symptoms in years yet I still see a psychotherapist once a month. This is due to the fact that the initial length of my suffering was extreme as I couldn't see the symptoms that I was exhibiting for myself - I couldn't recognize them on my own. I believe that it's absolutely necessary to continue with proactive measures to maintain a healthy psychological mindset.

This was a lesson hard learned, and I suffered a relapse because of it. The relapse prompted me to seek help again. I left the army in December 2017, getting an offer of employment with the Ottawa Police Service while I was training a group of future Close Protection Operators at the range of the Canadian Forces Base (CFB) in Borden, Ontario. I had applied to the Ottawa Police Service nearly two years earlier, knowing that I was suffering anxiety and burnout from my experiences and the workload I had allowed myself to shoulder while in the army. I thought, at the time, that a change in career would be the best thing for me and it would provide a break for my mental health and, perhaps, save my marriage. Spoiler alert: it didn't. I had been seeing a social worker regularly while in the army but when I did my honorable release to pursue a career in policing, I figured that I was leaving all my troubles behind me with the career change. That ignorance would bite me in the ass a year later.

I joined the Ottawa Police Services and went to the Ontario Police College for three months of training, as is mandatory for every single police officer hired in the province of Ontario. Part of the mandatory training is a session in an Olympic sized pool where officers must participate in mock rescue scenarios with a buoyant rescue tool (a donut or other similar item) – we rescue a partner and drag them back to shore. I did the training, but all I could think of the entire time I was acting as the 'person in distress' was that I was pretending to be a floating body in the Mediterranean Sea. The entire training lasted less than two hours but I was clearly uncomfortable the entire time. The instructor approached me afterwards, privately stating that they observed how uncomfortable I was, how I was rigid and had clenched fists. I've never been a bad swimmer, so I got that portion over with as fast as I could, but I hated the experience. I just kept thinking to myself that I wouldn't ever have to go through that again. In my mind, at the time, there was practically a zero percent chance that I was going to ever have to do anything with water as part of my job as a city cop. Boy, was I wrong.

Jesse Hewitt

After completing the training at the Ontario Police College, as well as my probationary 500 hours coach officer training with the Ottawa Police Service, I was cut loose to do calls by myself. I enjoyed the freedom immensely, it let me focus any downtime I had on pet projects. Some of these included coordinating with senior cops with their own connections to check on sex offenders to ensure they were abiding to their conditions, or doing walk-throughs of high-risk apartment buildings to show a police presence in order to help reduce risk of apartment takeovers.

I was working alone one shift in the summer, working a significant amount of overtime in order to afford a new house so that my family and I could upgrade from the townhouse we were living in at the time. My ex-wife (we hadn't divorced yet) had just given birth to our son and we needed to upgrade from our small house to a larger detached house which doubled the square footage. We made a family decision at the time that, while she was on maternity leave, that I would commit to as much overtime as possible in order to secure the down payment on the new build. This led me to the following situation.

Post-Traumatic Growth

Personal Anecdote
Flashbacks

A call for service was received one early afternoon requiring police response at beach nearby. A state of emergency had been declared in the city a couple weeks earlier due to high water levels along the Ottawa river. Uncommonly high levels of water had been recorded in the area due to extensive snowmelt during that spring. It had gotten so bad that the military had been deployed to a separate section of the city which had a suburb of houses on the shoreline. The water had risen so high that it was 76 meters above sea level, resulting in the flooding of entire suburbs - they were beneath water. The river was moving so fast that several kayakers in the early summer month of May had died or gone missing while on the Ottawa river. The rapids were moving so rapidly and violently that some bridges separating the provinces of Ontario and Quebec were forced to shut down entirely as water smashed into them and sprayed so high in the it disrupted safe traffic. The beach that the call originated from, and where assistance was required, had city bylaw officers set up at a control point to prevent anyone from swimming or launching boats in to the area.

The call details explained that there were five young adults, about 18-20yrs old, that had put an inflatable boat into the water, and who had in their possession various types of alcohol and a large purple bong for smoking marijuana. Bylaw officers had initially prevented them from putting the boat in the water, but they were found to have simply driven to the other side of the parking lot and quickly put the boat in and went on the water anyways. They didn't have life vests or paddles and they were about 30 feet from shore. Bylaw officers spent forty-five minutes ordering them to return to shore without success. The bylaw officers felt they had no choice but to phone the police for assistance. I arrived on scene prior to my partner and met with the two bylaw officers who were on scene. They explained what had happened as they brought me to the sandy beach. I hadn't been on a sandy beach since my tour in Libya, where I watched the bodies of men and women wash ashore, dead, on a sand beach such as this.

Jesse Hewitt

I called out to the group, with the two bylaw officers beside me, indicating that they needed to come to shore. I told them that people had died in these waters and that they had to come to shore immediately. I could see the group of them, four men and one woman huddled together in the boat. One of the men then called out to me saying that they weren't going to come in. I believe they said something along the lines of "Go fuck yourself". This fell in line with what the bylaw officers told me, as they were called "Rent a-cops", and "Losers" by the group prior to my arrival.

I could tell by the way the 'leader' was talking that he was inebriated at minimum. Now I was put in a position where I knew that the rapids were about 300 meters away from the boat, the water current was quickly moving in the group's direction, and they would inevitably get caught in that current because they didn't have paddles or life vests to try and combat it. In my mind, they were going to die unless an intervention was made immediately.

I told them one last time that if they didn't leave the water, I would come drag them out. I knew that thirty feet from shore the water was still shallow. Again, they refused to listen and at this point several of them had put their hands in the water to act as makeshift paddles trying to get further away from shore. I didn't have time to call for the fire department and we didn't have any boats available to intercept them before the group drifted towards the rapids due to the city-wide state of emergency. I refused to let these people die by floating into rapids, so I made the decision to get them to shore, whether they cooperated or not.

I waded out into the water, with all of my police gear still on. The gear, including belt, use of force items, vest and boots, added thirty pounds of weight to my person. I knew I wouldn't be able to swim with that amount of gear on, so I could only wade out as far as I could stand so as to not put myself at risk. I got out far enough to grab the side of the boat and put my hand on it to stop them from hand-paddling away. With the five people in the boat, and the boat itself heavy with the alcohol and a bong in it, it was too heavy for me to drag to shore. My boots were beginning to sink into the sand beneath the water and they

Post-Traumatic Growth

again refused when I told them to get out of the boat. At this point they met the grounds for arrest so I exercised that option.

I went to the closest male, whose back was to me. The water level was hitting my upper thighs now, and, with him being in a sitting position, he was sitting slightly taller than I was standing. I grabbed his left arm under the elbow with one hand and the wrist with the other, telling him to get out of the boat. He ripped his arm away and told me "Not to fucking touch him". I tried a second time with the same result. The third time I grabbed him, he was cocking his elbow preparing an attempt to assault me. I had enough, so I drew my conductive energy weapon (CEW), otherwise known as a taser, and with my other hand grabbed across his torso and pulled him out of the boat.

As part of the use of force teachings, to draw a CEW requires an assaultive subject. This subject was physically resisting arrest, risking both his life and four others, and had cocked his elbow in an attempt to hit me. Also, the initial draw of the CEW from the holster is an opportunity to gain compliance from the subject. It is not mandatory to deploy it, just like you don't have to shoot someone because you've drawn your firearm. These are steps in the use of force continuum we are taught when we go through Police College training, which allow the subjects opportunities to comply with the arrest. When I drew my CEW and pulled him from the raft, I pushed him toward shore, holstered my CEW and saw that the remaining four boaters got out of the boat and came to shore as well. The lone female in the group, whom I found out was the girlfriend of the subject I had pulled from the boat, decided to defend her man's honor, and pushed me on the chest. She was so drunk that she fell over backwards over a piece of driftwood. I warned her that if she touched me again, I would arrest her for assaulting a police officer.

I was not assaulted again, and by this time, my partner had arrived; he had been my former coach officer. The two of us obtained their names, issued appropriate tickets (without issuing the $5000 tickets for violating the emergency order in place for the river), and wrote the report. The entire incident took about 45 minutes from start to finish. I even obtained witness statements from the bylaw officers *detailing their entire interaction before and after police arrival. One of the men in the boat decided to record the entire exchange with his cellphone, and then uploaded an edited 45-minute encounter to a 53 second video on YouTube, which was edited to attack police officers by giving a negative portrayal of them. Such is the life of policing in today's society.*

What I didn't put in my written report was that when I went into the water, in my peripheral vision I saw bodies floating in the water. I knew they weren't there, because when I tried to focus and look at them, they were gone. It put a sick feeling in the pit of my stomach and I panicked. I believe if I wasn't suffering from issues with the water and having flashbacks, I likely would have been calmer and had more of a measured approach to the situation. I would have called for backup and for the fire department immediately, or asked for assistance downriver near the rapids those couple hundred meters away. The flashback inhibited me from being able to do my job effectively in the moment, and it caused me to overreact and panic internally.

I went home that night and had terrible nightmares. I relived that entire encounter but this time there were bodies floating in the water as I went to get the boat out, and as I went into the water, the bodies were grabbing at my legs. I was dragged into the water by them and I had an out-of-body experience in my dream where I was drowned, floating face-down in the water at that beach. I woke up covered in sweat, and I realized that my apprehension with water was still an issue, and felt it needed to be dealt with.

Post-Traumatic Growth

One of the methods I had used prior to the incident with the non-compliant boaters was exposure therapy. I engaged in exposure therapy while at the police academy and it helped me to become comfortable enough to go into the water. I decided to resume exposure therapy on my own, and it would later help me to overcome the flashbacks I experienced during policing. This was taught to me by not one mental health professional, but two. The social worker I met with initially in 2016, as well as my psychologist in 2019. Both mentioned the benefits of exposure therapy as an effective treatment for a post traumatic injury (PTSI). They each helped me with the setup and steps of how to expose myself to the negative stimulus, including the short period of time and moment of reflection after removing myself from it. I reported regularly during meetings to explain how the process went each time.

Exposure therapy is part of behavioural treatment for a post traumatic injury. It's inherently uncomfortable, because you're exposing yourself gradually to the triggers resulting from negative stimulus. The idea behind exposure therapy is to lessen a person's avoidance behaviour. Avoidance behaviour is exhibited when someone who is suffering from a post traumatic injury and is looking for a place of safety and protection from negative stimulus and potential triggers (Van Minnen, A., & Hagenaars, M. A. (2010)). This is absolutely understandable, because who would want to risk further injury? Bear with me though, because I have an analogy that will explain the risks of avoidance behaviour.

Imagine you're working on doing some refurbishing in your house and you step on a rusty nail sticking out from the floor. The first thing you'll want to do is get the weight off your foot, and then take a look at the damage. Turns out that getting weight off your foot helped with the pain. It's not bleeding that badly, so you wrap it up, pop some Tylenol and stay off your foot for the day. A week goes by and it's still hurting, so you take another look at it. At this point it looks infected, but now you're too embarrassed to go into the hospital to have it looked at, so you convince yourself to put some ointment on it, take some more Tylenol, and to keep staying off it. On top of the Tylenol, you crack a couple of beer to help numb the pain. Another week goes by and your foot feels numb rather than painful, so you figure the Tylenol and beer must be helping, so you decide to take more Tylenol. By the third week, you feel pretty groggy and you can smell something abnormal from your foot. You take your sock off to look underneath your foot and you can see green puss and black skin. By the time you go to the hospital, you've avoided taking care of it for so long that the doctors end up amputating at the ankle. Your avoidance behaviour and refusal to go to the hospital for treatment initially, and paying proper attention or exercising due diligence with the injury, led to the injury becoming much worse and resulting in much more serious treatment being required in response to the problem.

If you switch out the nail for a post-traumatic injury, the avoidance behaviour, as it becomes more extreme, will exacerbate the symptoms and eliminate your social support networks. For example, if a person suffering from a PTSI is out with their family at the park and a frisbee flies over their head without warning, it could trigger a ducking effect similar to when they experienced bullets whizzing by their temple. That situation could result in them staying at home and not leaving the house for weeks to avoid experiencing the trigger again.

That avoidance will only increase the level of reactivity the next time it happens however, and the avoidance inadvertently increases the effect of the symptoms related to the trigger. Avoiding situations that provoke particular thoughts and emotions may feel like stemming the flow of psychological pain and make you feel better in the short-term, but in fact, it is creating a threatening and dangerous platform in which your method of triaging symptomology soon becomes the rust that allows the infection to thrive. The purpose of exposure therapy is to prevent overexercising avoidance behaviour.

Post-Traumatic Growth

The Beginning of Exposure Therapy

When I participated in exposure therapy, I was somewhat lucky in the sense that my trigger – open bodies of water – was simple, as it is a physical, non-moving entity. If I wasn't comfortable going near water, I would simply stay away from it – done, in terms of avoidance behaviour. Some bodies of water bothered me and some didn't. It was outdoor bodies of water, specifically beaches, that I had trouble with. Even as I type this, I know that I am not ecstatic about going swimming this summer, but I know I'll do it because that's what I need to do in order to make sure I'm not crippled by my experiences. So, I continue to face large, open bodies of water and learn to manage the anxiety my memories give me.

There are several methods of exposure therapy, three of which I focused on myself: Imaginal, Interoceptive and in Vivo Exposure. It's important to recognize that exposure therapy is a single tool collected in, what should be, a large toolbox of mental health techniques that should be utilized to address symptoms and the heart of the injury or injuries. For example, it was found that 86% of clients who participated in prolonged exposure therapy had better outcomes than other in controlled conditions (Powers et al., 2010). That being said, although it is an effective treatment, 25-45% of individuals still met the diagnostic criteria for Post Traumatic Stress Disorder after treatment (Putnam et al., 1996). Post Traumatic Stress Disorder (PTSD) is very complicated and complex, resulting in the manifestation of the psychological issues years after the event or events occur, and usually is an amalgamation of several other psychological diagnoses (National Institute of Mental Health, 2021). These include but are not limited to PTSD, Alcohol Use Disorder, Anxiety, Suicidal Ideation, Homicidal Ideation, Depression, etc., (the diagnosis I was given). There is no 'universal fix' for all the injuries that encompass such a complex injury as PTSD. It took me utilizing several different social support services and networks concurrently in order to see progress in myself. I understand it sounds exhausting, and sometimes it is. I can attest that persistence and insight will pay off.

Jesse Hewitt

My initial exposure (In Vivo, which I'll explain next) was just thinking about going to the beach alone and sitting nearby. In Vivo exposure therapy is a form of Cognitive Behavior Therapy (CBT) that gradually exposes the person to the trauma by thinking about the memories that caused it and dealing with the symptoms. I let my body recognize the anxiety I was feeling considering going to the beach, because thinking about even going also brought on memories about *why* I was uncomfortable going there in the first place. I spoke to myself in my head about why I was going to go to the beach, and that there was nothing that was going to happen, and that the past was behind me. I practiced this several times a week, and afterwards I would calm myself and empty my mind by either going to do some hot yoga, or meditating if I didn't want to leave my house. The process of recalling the activity in my mind was an attempt to lessen the impact of the negative thoughts I had associated with going to the beach or being near water. I considered it at the time like I was kind of 'psyching myself up' before going on a mission, about to go for a personal best on a weightlift, or jumping out of an airplane with a parachute. Once I was comfortable with having the thoughts of the beach, I decided that it was time to expose myself to seeing it in person.

I then began Interoceptive Exposure. Interoceptive exposure sets out to bring on the physical sensations (somatic) instead of simply the memories of the stress. The focus would be on the symptom I was experiencing, such as the increased heartrate being a precursor to an anxiety attack. I was reexperiencing the physical symptoms of the psychological trauma in order to acclimatize myself to them so they no longer hurt me. It was extremely distressing, and reliving those feelings as well as the memories was difficult and sickening to my stomach. The goal was that there would be a reduction in future anxiety or panic attacks in the future. Once I worked through Interoceptive Exposure, I evolved into allowing myself to be physically present in front of a trigger. I allowed myself to introduce stimulus in order to create a heightened mental threshold to tolerate my anxiety and increase the limit of tolerance to reduce the negative reaction to become more successful in future encounters with the beach.

Post-Traumatic Growth

My first time out I went to a private beach and sat on a rock nearby. I watched as the water flowed in and out peacefully on a summer day. I sat for about thirty minutes without any stimulus nearby at all – the area was absent of other people on the beach and with no boats or people in the water. If they were present, they were at a good distance. By all accounts, it was a beautiful day. I did this gradually and, eventually, I increasingly allowed myself to walk along the beach, and then walk with my feet in the water. My purpose behind this was to eliminate the negative experiences by simply outnumbering it with more positive experiences in a similar physical setting. It was a focus of repetition, gradually increasing my involvement while diminishing the discomfort of the beach. It was difficult in the evenings sometimes, as it was taxing mentally and I would be exhausted after exposing myself to that stimulus. As I got more comfortable with the beach, I brought my dog and let him swim in the water, which was a hurdle for me. It was one thing to be at the beach alone, it was another thing entirely to watch something splash and disturb that peace. I went home after that and had nightmares that evening. I learned that although I was tackling the subject matter that was a trigger for me, within that subject matter were needles of sharp memories or what I call micro-triggers which flare up the entire symptom again if stepped on carelessly.

I maintained that form exposure therapy in police college, going swimming on my own inside the indoor pool and then with other cadets at the same time. Those were more uncomfortable, as the bodies splashing around me created a sense that I had lost control of the situation I was exposing myself too. I would go to sleep at night and have nightmares about the beach, even though it was just a pool with people in it. I continued this exposure therapy until I graduated the police college. Afterwards, I went to swim lessons with my son, but that was the extent of my personal exposure therapy for over a year. That delay in exposure therapy resulted in a relapse for me, because I was not prepared for what happened when I dragged those people out of the boat during the state of emergency. I had been allowing avoidance behaviour to take over because I thought I had dealt with the issue. I was wrong, and now I don't take post-traumatic therapy for granted anymore.

I mentioned previously that healing from post-traumatic psychological injuries must be maintained and treated similarly to how physiotherapy treats an injured ligament. Simply stopping treatment will allow the mental injury to tighten and risks relapse, just like letting your injured ligaments tear or rupture without a plan to treat the future health of the injured body part. In allowing myself to practice avoidance behaviour for that period of time, I believe I relapsed because I had allowed my psychological injury to become tightened into an inflexible ball again. Without the exposure therapy giving me the practiced consistency of being in and around water, I was not mentally resilient to the impact of another negative stimulus related to a beach and people in water. That negligence for my mental health impacted me both personally and professionally.

Avoidance behaviour allowed a relapse to occur, so I decided to start the exposure therapy fresh again. Now I had two compounding negative experiences with water, so I started first by imagining going to the beach and then, after time passed, beginning the gradual exposure to the physical components that were part of the issue. After I did this, I again went to the private beach, at first by myself, then eventually with my dog again and then with my current wife. She knows about my trauma and is the strongest social support I have, which made the experience easier than simply bringing a friend.

Since that time, I've brought my children to the beach swimming and I've gone to public beaches myself with my wife and friends. I no longer suffer the crippling effects of that injury and I've largely gotten past it. With all injuries however, I'm cautiously optimistic about exposing myself to triggers that no longer bother me. I won't take for granted that the symptoms are removed from my consciousness forever, because I believe that's an ignorant frame of mind and every person who has suffered from a PTSI should be mindful and wiser going forward in their lives.

Chapter 5
Anxiety & Panic Attacks

I heard about panic attacks and anxiety attacks before I ever experienced one. I heard that a panic attack will trigger such a sense of overwhelming doom that you'll feel as if you're about to die. I had seen it happen with family members of mine who were war veterans before joining the army myself. I experienced one for the very first time while I was cooking dinner in the kitchen on a regular, boring night. This was in 2016, before I had sat down with a social worker. At this point in my life, I was drinking most nights when I got home from work, then playing online games with my coworkers if I wasn't working late or on an operation. I'd typically bring my service pistol home and just leave it in my holster on my living room table and head downstairs. I was emotionless and withdrawn from friends and family. I was simply going through the motions at work as well as at home. I would get unreasonably angry at small things, and even though I would verbally acknowledge that I was angry, I also knew that it would take me the entire day to calm down. I had become in-tune with myself to the point where I knew once I had reached the point of anger it would carry with me and effect my mood for hours on end. I didn't have the ability to reflect upon *why* I was so angry though, just like I couldn't reflect upon why I was emotionally numb.

On the night in question, I stood over the stove and my heart began to beat. Quickly. It was beating so hard it felt like I should be able to see it outside of my chest. I knew something was wrong, and I had to reach out to hold on to the counter because I didn't know if I was having a heart attack or not. I was terrified about what was happening to me, and I didn't know if I'd even have the strength and coordination to call for help if I needed to. Part of my job was remaining physically fit, and every member of the unit I was with worked out for a two-hour block of time per day. It felt like my body was betraying me and I didn't know what to do. I looked over myself to make sure I wasn't injured and tried to think about why my body would be acting this way. It felt like I was losing complete control of myself, and I hated it.

I sat down until I was able to calm down and my heart stopped beating as if it was going to burst out of my chest. I couldn't make sense of why I had experienced an anxiety attack, especially without stimulus or a trigger. That confusion about not being able to pinpoint *why* I was having the anxiety attack made me panic even more. I wasn't sure if I was having a heart attack or if I was going to pass out. I eventually calmed down after sitting on the floor, covered in sweat. I knew I needed help and it was shortly after that night when I went to my first appointment with a social worker through the army medical center.

The most surprising thing about the anxiety I experienced was that it never happened while I was on-shift working. I could be in the middle of an operation overseas, conducting live-fire CQB training, or taking a domestic call as a cop, yet the anxiety only ever hit me when in situations where everything was calm. It's like my body was on autopilot when doing those high-intensity operations. I found when I was at home, I was at risk of having them more often because I found I was reflecting on the past. I would be thinking about the most recent operation, or call I had attended, and suddenly the anxiety would well up within me. It crept up my spine and my gut and I couldn't shake it once it set in. I had to ride the wave until it subsided, and it was a horrible feeling. I felt like my body and mind betrayed me, and I felt ashamed and weak afterwards. I would get so exhausted from the

Post-Traumatic Growth

attacks sometimes that I would need to go lay down for hours afterwards.

I learned a lot about what I was experiencing from the social worker I met with. I learned that I was having panic attacks in my sleep. I generally don't remember most of my dreams, and that continues to this day. The few dreams I would recall were nightmares about what I had experienced overseas. Those specific dreams I would have several times a week, with varying degrees of differences or perspectives in them. If it wasn't water related dreams, it would be one of a few others that happened on land that haunted me deeply at the time. Those dreams were always influenced by real life memories, including the one outlined in the next passage.

Jesse Hewitt

Personal Anecdote
Difficult Choices

In 2014, as the civil war in Libya affected what little stability the country had left, other countries began ordering their citizens to close and evacuate the embassies operating within the city. To name a few, but not all, these countries would include Great Britain, Germany, United States of America, Canada, and Japan. We, Canada, were one of the last countries to evacuate, and did so after the USA had completed their evacuation. At that point we had little in the way of neighbouring support and the fighting in the country was at an all time high.

By this point in the mission, the local militias had driven tanks onto the Tripoli International Airport and shot all of the passenger airline planes with tank and mortar fire. Within hours they leveled an entire international airport. I saw the smoke rising from the burning airport, and nearby oilfields that were ablaze, all from the rear door of my apartment. The entire city was covered in a haze of choking smoke, and you could hardly breathe without gasping due to the fumes in the air. Gunfire was happening 24/7 in the distance and our surgeon was shot at while son her balcony, this is on video as she was recording the fighting in the distance from her cellphone. You could hear the rounds whizzing in and hitting the wall beside her. We had to duck in our backyard as bullets flew overhead. We did rotated shifts and had to 'hardpoint' (A safe place to hunker down temporarily) the ambassador in his residence for days at a time, all the while watching what looked like a scene in a Star Wars movie from the tracer fire. Only a couple of miles away the fighting was obviously intense with the amount of tracer fire in the air. Tracer fire is a type of ammunition that has a chemical that burns brightly when fired. The military uses it to track the trajectory of bullets at night, adjusting as necessary. After some coordination and a recce however, we did a move to the embassy from our living quarters, a little over twenty kilometers west, with members of the Close Protection team. We emptied out all sensitive information from the building.

Post-Traumatic Growth

What we couldn't bring with us we destroyed and then we sealed the door.

A member of the team coordinated with the British embassy security forces (SAS) and did a joint recce of the road west of Tripoli into the neighbouring country of Tunisia (About 420 kilometers away). Once that was done, members of the Close Protection Team were tasked with drafting the Operation Orders, which detailed the process for evacuation of all embassy personnel and sensitive equipment out of the country. We had six armored vehicles to transport the team, all personnel, and equipment. Each member was tasked with a responsibility, and mine was the armored vehicles. I had a contact within the city that was the mechanic for the team and, with his help, I ensured the vehicles were operational for the twenty-three-hour move while carrying all the equipment.

I anticipated as much as I could and we tied extra run-flat (a tire that when deflated has a hard plastic insert that allows it to drive off the rim for a short period of time) tires to the roof, as well and put bright red tape in a symbol on it (Like a big red letter "T"). The symbol had significance, as well as the cellphones we were given immediately before the move. These phones were connected with a specific email address, and we all had the same account. The account was being monitored by the United States Air Force (USAF), and anything drafted in that email would be monitored. The cellphones also sent out the GPS coordinates to the USAF, who had an airborne drone following us and ensuring they had the right vehicles. They were able to track the correct vehicles thanks to the marking of the bright red tapes on the roof of each of the armored trucks.

We departed before dawn, after prepping as much as possible and spreading the diplomatic staff between vehicles to ensure that at least two Close Protection members were with each vehicle in case of an incident. The fighting had occurred and escalated over Ramadan, and gotten so bad by the summer months that the roadways were deserted by civilians. Gas was nearly non-existent and there were extreme food shortages. Oil storage depots were completely aflame, and the smoke was so heavy across the city that you couldn't manage anything but shallow breaths and we had constant headaches. Rival militias would drag debris to block vehicles or set a wall of tires that had been dragged across the roadway aflame.

We were lucky that the normal sets of flaming tires on the roads weren't there that morning, otherwise we'd have to try and clear them. We managed to exit out of the Tripoli city limits past Janzur and Surman and into the rural areas without contact with any enemy militias or Ansar al-Sharia. The convoy was met without incident until about four hours into the evacuation road move. We were on a 'paved' road in the Libyan desert (part of the Sahara Desert), which has average daytime temperatures of 50 degrees Celsius, or 122 degrees Fahrenheit. There were no shoulders on the road, rather, loose desert sands on the edges. We saw little in the way of vehicle traffic and only a few wild camels here and there. At one point, a small sedan was driving behind the convoy. We had our six vehicles in a loose convoy to prevent significant casualties if we hit an IED. The car passed two of the vehicles, with the vehicle I was driving being the last car her passed. The sedan was being driven by a single male driver of local nationality. He cut in front of my vehicle so quickly that, before I could consider ramming him off the road, the front right tire of the sedan hit the loose sand on the shoulder. The vehicle overcorrected and spun out on the right side of the road. The convoy stopped momentarily as two of the vehicles were being driven by support staff members of the mission, and did not think to simply drive on and leave the sedan to its fate. We had given them instructions prior to the evacuation on how to react to any attack on the convoy, to no avail. They cannot be blamed however, as the circumstances were so extraordinary that none of the pre-deployment training prepared for this level of threat on the support staff.

We had a Canadian interpreter with us who spoke Arabic, but struggled to understand the Libyan dialect fluently. I watched as he approached the driver with one of our operators and recognized that the driver was going ballistic, screaming and yelling at us. This was typical behaviour, as it was my experience that the male Libyans were very animated when provoked. What I did not expect was our inter-

Post-Traumatic Growth

preter to suddenly run back to the armored truck, open his door and grab his pistol, racking a round in the chamber. We had no idea what was said, and after calming him down, he told us that the man was yelling that he was going to call and get his uncle, who is a part of the local militia, to kill us for ruining his car - his tires had blown out when he skidded into the sand, leaving it totally disabled.

We were suddenly put in a difficult position. He was a potential combatant, but at the current moment, he was not a threat. We were not in a position to simply kill the man because it didn't meet the rules of engagement – not to mention the fact that we had a convoy of civilian diplomatic staff watching from the armored vehicles. Shooting the unarmed man in the middle of the desert would have put us all in jail for the rest of our lives. The taskforce determined that the best course of action, in order to get us out of that area and into Tunisia as fast as possible, was to put several thousand Dinar in a briefcase, give it to him and let him brave the Libyan Desert heat. We were several hours drive in either direction to the nearest chunk of civilization, and nobody had cell service. That man wasn't calling anyone, and he was stuck in the desert with a briefcase full of Ghaddafi marked currency and we left him to behind in the heat. We left him in the heat without anything except a wrecked vehicle and a briefcase of cash.

Now, I don't know if you've ever experienced heat like that in the desert, but it's crippling. Fifty plus degrees, even hotter in a car that isn't running. Windex would steam off the widows instantly on contact when I would try to clean them in the summer heat. I had no doubt that the man was being given money to die alone in the desert. The convoy loaded back up after the man was given the briefcase full of cash and was left to his fate in the Libyan Desert, with no help in sight. I would estimate he only had a couple hours survivability in that heat without shade or water. Presumably, he succumbed to the heat and died.

Jesse Hewitt

One of the few nightmares I had consistently were themed with walking in that desert heat with a briefcase in my hand. I would walk for what seemed like hours in the sand before collapsing dead. There was no panic in the dreams, but a massive sense of deep life-threatening dread, like a sense of hopelessness and certainty of death. I would wake up with my bed soaked in sweat, feeling physically weak, with my heart beating out of my chest. I would stay awake for hours after that, unable to shake that feeling of dread in my soul. Sometimes, I would fight so hard in my sleep that I would end up fighting myself awake. Other times, I would get injured in my dream and feel what I can best describe as the 'ghosts' of those injuries for days after waking up. One dream in particular was of a bullet hitting me in the back of the head – it felt as if the back of my head was empty, had water splashed on it and was running down the back of my neck the entire next day. I knew nothing was wrong with my head, and that it was just a dream, but I could still feel warm liquid rolling down the back of my neck.

With the anxiety and panic attacks haunting me in both my waking and sleeping hours, I could not catch a break. I reached out to my mom who lived several provinces away at the time to ask her if she could fly to my house and spend a couple weeks at home with me. I told her I needed the support and she arrived within a week. I had access to unlimited benefits regarding any psychologist I needed to talk to. The army would pay for them to see me, but it was on me to find someone.

At this point in 2016 I was suffering greatly. I was overexercising at work; overcommitting myself; drinking most nights, bulimic (which I realized was an attempt at controlling something in my life with the binging and purging); not sleeping most of the time and, when I did, I soaked the bed with sweat, fighting in my sleep and waking up to the sheets being torn off the bed, staring off into the distance or daydreaming; having memory issues, either emotionless or full of rage; and a slew of other issues. I knew by this point I needed help, and as emotionally deadpan as I was at the time, I was getting brittle and I knew I was in for a total breakdown. My thoughts had become intrusive and were impacting my career and daily routines. I needed to learn

Post-Traumatic Growth

to manage those intrusive thoughts in order to focus on the positives in my life. I had to understand that no matter how trained psychologically, physically, and regardless of strength of will, it's possible that mental health struggles can affect anyone… including myself.

Chapter 6
Managing Intrusive Thoughts of Homicidal Ideation

When I was going through my divorce, my ex-wife stole my Veterans Affairs diagnosis that included a breakdown of the PTSD, Homicidal and Suicidal Ideation, Alcohol Use Disorder, and Severe Depression Diagnoses. The fourteen-page report, detailing the worst things I was feeling over my time within the military, was suddenly read aloud in family court – on the record – without my permission. It was a *total* violation. This wrongdoing therefore made it available for the world to look up and read. I was mortified that the deeply personal document was available for the world to see. To make things worse, the media got wind of it and then published an article stating that an Ottawa Police Officer shouldn't be employed when he was diagnosed with PTSD and that he should never have been hired in the first place. Since that document became public, every time I've gone to testify as a police witness (before and after retiring) I've spent an average of five hours of cross examination, each time, being grilled over my mental health even though it had nothing to do with the case being argued. I've been accused of being drunk while at work, trying to hurt people, forgetting information, and otherwise simply being too ill to properly do my job. Each time I was on the stand I defended myself calmly, refusing to allow someone else, someone who was being paid to attack me, to rile me up. It was difficult, but I knew the environment I was going into. I was mentally exhausted at the end of each day of testimony, but I expected as much. Though, this should have never been the case to begin with.

I've written earlier how a lack of mental preparedness and significant break in therapy opens up the opportunity for a relapse in symptoms related to the PTSI. I allowed that to happen to myself with both Exposure Therapy, as well as the Cognitive Behavioural Therapy I underwent, which I'll explain shortly. Before I go into detail however, it's important for non-first responder readers to understand homicidal and suicidal ideation.

Suicidal ideation is the thoughts of harming yourself or ending your life. People that experience the loss of a loved one, victims of abuse, financial stress, feelings of isolation, depression, or who are suffering from legal battles, all have increased likelihood of suicidal ideation (Blais et al., 2023). First responders can be exposed to all the things any other civilian would, but also have the added stress of a career marinated in extreme emotion, adrenaline, conflict, life or death situations, and trauma. Firefighters, Emergency Medical Services (EMS), and police officers have increased risk of suicidal ideation compared to other non-first responder careers, with police officers suffering suicidal ideation at nearly 30% within their lifetime (Abbot et al., 2015). The same study also shows a correlation between suicidal ideation with depression and anger. Police officers that admitted to burnout suffered greater than their peers, with 117% greater likelihood of suicidal ideation (Bishop and Boots, 2014).

Burnout is a state of physical, emotional, and mental exhaustion caused by long-term stress, leading to a negative impact in job performance and mental and physical health problems. Although first responders are at a greater risk to experience suicidal ideation, it's common across other non-first responder careers and isn't indicative of imminent plans of suicide. In my case, I was diagnosed while still an actively patrolling police officer. If the psychologist thought I was in imminent danger of self-harm, they would have stopped me from going back to a career where I strapped a gun to my hip every day. That didn't happen, and through therapy I dealt with the issues that were creating the suicidal ideation and became a healthier person over time.

Homicidal ideation is the thoughts of homicide. It can range from vague ideas to detailed, well thought out plans **without** actually committing the act. It's also extremely common, with one study conducted by Kenrick and Sheets (1993) of a group of undergraduate students reporting that 79% of men and 53% of women reported homicidal ideation at least once in their lifetime (Kenrick and Sheets, 1993). That mindset, just like suicidal ideation, does not mean that the thoughts of hurting someone automatically means it's a precursor to the act itself. I would argue that it is normal to have homicidal ideations, depending on the circumstances. Men and women in the military, and other similar careers such as police, are trained to scan the area they are in and plan for conflict, and prepare mentally for it. In a warzone, homicidal ideation is a normality, because soldiers must be prepared to respond with lethal action if the situation demands it. I'd go so far as to state that it is a requirement. That training is engrained into both soldiers and police officers. Entering rooms and scanning for threats is part of the job, and preparing for conflict as well. It simulates a fight or flight response, and both soldiers and police officers are trained to always fight, and never allow themselves to flee from conflict. It is necessary for those two careers to think to the extremes of homicidal ideation, when the situation demands it. If a police officer did rise to the utmost severity of intrusive thoughts (homicidal ideations) that means he or she would be blindly and naively walking their beat (patrolling their zone) without taking into consideration all the information coming in. They would be so impacted with the psychological injury (homicidal ideations) that they would not be consciously able to utilize the OODA Loop which would allow them the tactical advantage over their adversary. Without thinking in the tactical mindset, when a life-threatening stimulus arises, they would be placed in a position to simply fire blindly with their firearm, without taking any consideration of the consequences, or planning for that eventuality.

What needs to happen in situations that have the potential to rise to the level of grave physical harm, or death, to the police officer or soldier, is to keep their priorities in check. In that situation, a clear priority is to ensure that they survive and protect the lives of bystanders. A way for a person in this role to do this is to plan to commit a legal homicide as a last resort. People react more quickly to stimulus if they are prepared for it and have envisioned the outcome. If a police officer plans, and takes into consideration the potential for each combatant to be hiding a weapon, in the vicinity or close enough that it is capable of harming a victim, or posing a risk to themselves or others in a life-threatening manner, that cop needs to plan (unfortunately) to draw their firearm and shoot until the threat is stopped. Homicidal ideation is deeply engrained in the training for careers of armed first responders. There is a reason that police officers are only trained to shoot at the center of mass of a body (the torso), because it's the easiest and most effective place to shoot a person to get them to stop, quite literally, dead in their tracks.

In my experience, seeing it through myself and my peers as both a soldier and a police officer, the mentality of scanning for threats, assessing potential combative situations/ambushes and ultimately preparing mentally with homicidal ideation, is carried from those careers into their personal lives. Preparing one's mind against the potential of lethal ambushes on cops/soldiers, attending calls for service that involve extreme violence, or going into a warzone all engrain the mentality of homicidal ideation. It's extremely difficult to simply "shut off" work when coming home from an environment like that, especially when your life depends on it. For longer serving members, and for members who have suffered from psychological injuries that unbending 'work until you die' mentality becomes engrained into their character and they unconsciously begin scanning for threats or checking the corners of rooms when entering restaurants. Another behaviour is to always sit in a seat facing the entrance door to see who is coming in. It's important to acknowledge this behaviour and become aware of the reasons why you're doing it. Unless you're in a high-crime area, there is no reason to sit facing the entrance of the restaurant or to assume there are potential combatants in the area while off-duty. Every-day-life isn't a fight or flight scenario, and it's incredibly important for your mental health and the health of your family to be aware of that.

Due to the psychological injuries of burnout, depression, PTSD, alcohol misuse disorder, etc., I suffered from both suicidal and homicidal ideation at the same time. I was constantly in fight or flight response and the career I was in at the time worked counter to being able to improve my mental health. I recognized that I was searching for conflict as a way to get both an adrenaline rush and to fuel those negative suicidal/homicidal tendencies. I'll speak to an example next.

Post-Traumatic Growth

Personal Anecdote
Trigger Warning – Violence

I had just started night shift at 9pm as a cop. I was in the station catching up on some reports from the shift prior. At about 9:10pm I heard dispatch on my radio calling out that an armed robbery had just occurred down the road from me. The call details were coming in quickly, and the information that immediately came in was that there were three black men, mid 20s, in masks that had just robbed a man and woman in front of a convenience store with a sawed-off shotgun. The man had been stabbed in the leg. All of the couple's items were stolen and they had made the 911 call inside the convenience store.

That patrol zone where the call took place wasn't the zone I had been assigned to that evening, so I asked dispatch if they needed additional units to help. They attached me to the call immediately so I hopped in my cruiser and threw on my emergency lights before racing to the scene. Just prior to my arrival, another officer went into the convenience store to talk to the victims and await an ambulance. I knew the area well, and I knew the best bet to catch the subjects was to establish what is referred to as an "outer cordon", which is kind of like a circle around a crime scene but pushed further out around the area. I called dispatch to see if any K9 officers were available to start a track of the subjects and set myself up.

I knew that a visible police presence would scare them off or hunker them down, so I shut off my exterior and interior lights and parked near a parking lot behind the convenience store, looking in to the store. My plan was to wait for K9 to arrive, assist with the track and hopefully find the subjects or at least the stolen items. More information was coming in through dispatch as the secondary officer was speaking with the victims and updating officers that were on the call over the radio. Now the details were three or four black men, with masks, a sawed-off shotgun, a knife and possibly a taser. They stole cellphones, a purse, a wallet, and a backpack from the victims.

As I sat in my vehicle, about twenty meters away, I saw two figures walking from the north side of the convenience store toward me and the

Jesse Hewitt

parking lot. There were several vehicles in the parking lot and they didn't see me at first. There were street lights overhead that illuminated them enough to see that the two men were about mid 20's and darker skinned, matching the vague description given to me over the radio. The vehicle they approached was facing away from me with the passenger side facing me. I saw the shorter of the two males approach the rear driver side door, take off a dark backpack and toss it into the car before closing the door. The taller male opened the front passenger door at the same time and, just before they both got into the vehicle, the short male on the driver's side saw me over the roof of the car. The two of them exchanged looks, shut the doors and began walking away from the car. I got out of my cruiser and yelled at them to stop and put their hands up.

 I should have drawn my firearm at that point and ordered them to the ground, then called for backup. I had two of three (or more) subjects and had every reason to believe that, at least one of them, had a firearm, a knife and a taser. The description of a sawed-off shotgun was enough for me know that my life was in danger as well as the life of any member of the public nearby. A shotgun would go through my Kevlar vest and the subjects were already known for extreme violence based on the 911 call information. Again, I should have drawn my gun... but I didn't. Those suicidal and homicidal ideations had impacted how I was conducting myself on the job and it impacted what I did next. I found myself in a position where I could roll the dice and see if I could get myself killed or kill the enemy in front of me. I hated myself and everyone around me, and if I could find a stimulus this dangerous, the opportunity to end my pain or set them up in a position where I could utilize the homicidal ideation to its ultimate fruition. The situation could then have been the chance to do so. I was setting myself up in a position where I was either going to be fast enough to stop myself from getting killed, or I'd die, and I was giving them a head start.

 I approached them, telling them to get their hands in the air, and they complied. As I approached, I recognized the taller male as someone I had arrested a month earlier for threatening to kill a secu-

Post-Traumatic Growth

rity guard at a local college nearby. He wasn't a student at the college, preferring a life of violent crime instead, and within the last month had been arrested and released for impaired driving. I could see it in his eyes that he recognized me from the incident a month earlier. With their hands still in the air, I approached them, waiting to see if either of them would reach to their waistline for a weapon. They didn't move and just stared at me. I informed them, in no uncertain terms, that if either of them wanted their legacy to be a dead body in a dark parking lot, the only thing they had to do was lower their hands. Neither of them moved and I realized at that point that the likelihood of them trying to kill me was decreasing, and that the gun was either in the car or I was about to be ambushed by the outstanding subject that I couldn't see.

I couldn't arrest them at this time. Going hands-on with two subjects, with an unlocated gun and a third subject that could very well ambush me with a gun, a knife or a taser, kept me from grabbing two sets of handcuffs from my belt immediately. I did a quick pat down of their waistline and didn't feel any bulging weapons. I asked the short male what he threw into the car. He denied doing anything of the sort. I demanded the keys to the vehicle, which I saw were in his left hand, still high above his head. I took the keys from his hand and backed up slowly to the door that he opened earlier. I did this in order to remain facing them in case either tried to attack me or draw a weapon that I hadn't located on them a moment earlier. I saw the black bag laying across the back seats and picked it up. It was heavy, and as I unzipped the first couple inches of the top of the bag, I saw the butt of a sawed-off gun, and a bloody knife nearby. I closed the door and told both men they were under arrest. They complied without incident, and after they were taken away by other officers who arrived on scene seconds later, I took the firearm out of the bag. I unloaded it and found a live round (bullet) in the chamber.

I didn't realize I hadn't drawn my gun because of the suicidal/homicidal ideations until over a year later. It took time to come to terms with myself and what my actions were leading to. It's like I was on a train track barreling ahead and I couldn't go anywhere but the final destination, which was the end of me.

Coming to terms with that and taking responsibility for both my thoughts and behaviour is part of cognitive behaviour therapy. It took time, introspection, and humility to come to terms with myself. Frankly, it was one of the final and most enlightening parts of the therapy I was going through. In high-threat jobs where decisions often have severe consequences, people that are suffering from psychological injury are unable to take criticism without becoming extremely defensive. I found that I was fighting and justifying every single one of my actions, and I couldn't be convinced otherwise. I became full of anger, and it blinded me to what I was thinking and how I was behaving. Looking back on those times now, I don't blame myself for those actions and thoughts, because they were coming from a sick man. Instead, I empathize with him. Having gone through significant hardships, trials, and challenges to my physical and mental health, I am forever grateful that I was able to receive help and come out healthier. Once I came to terms with my condition(s) and then worked on eliminating the symptoms, I began to feel healthier and take the first steps in a journey to improved mental health. I share personal trials and tribulations in this book hoping to help others who are in the middle of their anger. People that need to take a step back determine if their anger, depression, burnout, and helplessness are feelings they want to feel the rest of their lives. Mental health injuries can be treated, but the hardest part is taking the first step forward in recovery from a dead stop.

Chapter 7
The Right Professional for You

It's incredibly important to find a mental health professional that you connect with and are comfortable speaking to. Whether it's a psychiatrist, psychologist, psychotherapist, mental health nurse, social worker, counsellor, or religious figure, you won't be able to allow yourself to get better if you don't trust them to hear you and help you. Once trust is established, you can begin to soften the barriers you've erected around your psyche and allow some of that pain out in order to receive treatment for the injuries you're suffering from. Don't be afraid to ask questions about what kind of experience they have, their qualifications and what kind of treatment they provide. For example, I was hesitant to be prescribed with any medication because I've seen friends who were suffering have severe side effects from medications. Not to mention that getting off some medications can be a struggle itself because they need to be weaned off – it can cause severe issues stopping medications cold turkey. I was open and honest about my hesitation, should a psychologist or psychiatrist want to provide medication. I asked that, prior to those decisions being made, we expend every available option. Some possibilities include meditation, yoga, group therapy, or just about anything else. I was open to whatever they wanted. In the end, I learned about Dialectical Behavioural Therapy, Cognitive Behavioural

Therapy, and several other treatment options that I will explain later in this book. The combination of these treatment options, as well as an incredible support network, enabled me the ability to not require medication. Mental health injuries are never simply gone forever once the symptoms subside, and if there is suitable medication I require in the future, then I'll gladly take it.

I struggled at first to find a mental professional I connected with. It took me some time, but I eventually found several mental health professionals that worked for me for the various issues I was suffering from. Although I was unsure, after speaking with these professionals, I was humbled after realizing that they were the experts in their field, similar to how I was the expert in my field of work. I needed to lose any ego going into these meetings, and drop the idea that those men and women I was reaching out to for help were not prepared for what I was suffering from.

I reached out initially to several civilian psychologists in the area, hoping to avoid driving the 45 minutes across town to see the social worker at the military hospital. The few I met were not a fit for me. I walked into one establishment and met with an older woman who had short, dyed-pink hair and had framed pictures of cats in her office. The environment was too off-putting for me, and I very nearly laughed in her face and told her she wasn't prepared for what I was going to tell her. I did a short introduction for thirty minutes and cut out of the meeting early.

I met with several male civilian psychologists, ranging in age from early 40's to late 60's. They were okay, but something prevented me from feeling a connection with them, and I couldn't find myself trusting or having a rapport with them. I ultimately found a connection with a female social worker at the military hospital. She had the 'matter of fact' and straightforward personality I resonated with. I'm generally more of a 'stand-off' type guy at first when talking about anything related to my mental health. However, after several hours with her, I started to go into detail about some of my issues. I felt comfortable around her because she presented professionally, didn't cock her eyebrow at anything I was saying, or gasp at anything I confided either. The most significant feeling I had was that I knew she *believed me*. One of my biggest fears at the time was that no one would believe I was injured. I struggled to come to terms with it myself because I couldn't *see* the injury. I was thankful, however, as in those meetings with her I was met with respect and understanding by the social worker. She was amazing. She even went so far as to take time to point out to me how I would physically do certain things like squeeze my trigger finger, or constantly tap my heel on the ground because I was manifesting the stress outwardly. She helped me recognize the signs of anxiety and panic attacks as they were unfolding in my life. She was an honest and helpful person and she ended up diagnosing me with my first mental health issue: Adjustment Disorder with Anxiety.

Just like many PTSI's occur from cumulative experiences, I would say they are especially so for first responders who see similar horrible incidents more frequently. A study by Douglas Bremner and his colleagues showed strong evidence that repeated exposure to traumatic events can lead to cumulative harm and increased risk of mental health injuries like PTSD and depression (Bremner et al., 2006). The continual grind of negative stimuli will lead to inevitable change in personality, such as what many refer to as 'dark humor.' Dark humor makes light of subjects or incidents that are too taboo to discuss openly. First responders generally make use of dark humor in response to horrible incidents occurring in front of them as a mechanism to cope with the negative stimulus. It's an extremely common form of expression in the roles of first responders, including paramedics, fire fighters, police officers, nurses, doctors and soldiers. Topics of dark humor can include sudden deaths, poverty, stereotypes, discrimination, etc. It's not a type of humor that is easily understood and is not typically condoned outside of emergency services. I would say it's been unacceptable by policy for years already. Many careers have 'inside jokes' that relate to the profession, and those jokes, depending on the career, can be morbid, obscene, and very dark compared to a desk job. For example, I went to a call where a woman had abandoned her infant baby in a stroller outside of her house. It was a rainy, cool May afternoon. I arrived on scene, rescued the baby, and arrested the woman for child abandonment. I found out during the investigation that she had opened a neighbours' door and ushered her two other toddler aged children inside, assuming the neighbour would take care of them. The Children's Aid Society of Ottawa arrived and seized all three children into their care. It's a horrible situation where nobody wins, but one of the officers on scene made a quip about "at least the arrested mother wouldn't have to worry about paying for babysitting anymore". I chuckled at the audacity of what he said and carried on with my report. Dark humor happens, and although it's taboo, I find it's nearly a necessity for first responders to cope with the negative stimuli they're exposed to so often in their careers.

These cumulative incidents of stressful events cannot simply be coped with by peers making light of situations with dark humor alone. Negative stimuli accumulate and, for many people, cause psychological injuries. Substance Abuse and Mental Health Services Administration (SAMHSA) released a report in 2018 which shows that upwards of 30% of first responders suffer from Post Traumatic Stress Disorder (PTSD), and that first responders are ten times more likely to contemplate suicide (Abbot et al., 2015). It's also extremely important to remember that PTSD stemming from Post Traumatic Stress Injuries (PTSIs, also known as Operation Stress Injuries, or OSI's) is more commonly diagnosed given the more social supports that exist to offer care and service. Post Traumatic Stress injuries are extremely prevalent in careers such as those of first responders, and those that have post-traumatic injuries are forced to suffer in silence if there are not appropriate social support structures in place to help them. I want to note that every single person on earth, (including animals!) can suffer the symptoms associated with PTSD. There is no level of resilience that makes anyone immune to the effects of stress and trauma. It can happen to any person, regardless of career, age, or background. I focus my attention to first responders because that's what I know from my previous careers, but it's important to remember that anyone can be susceptible to the effects of trauma physically, and psychologically. Domestic abuse survivors, sexual assault survivors, victims of violent accidents,

Post-Traumatic Growth

and individuals who have observed traumatic events, all regularly suffer from depression, anxiety, suicidal ideation and more, here I am simply naming a few.

I have personally observed that training on mental resiliency has become part of the structured training in both the military and in civilian policing. Both the Military and Municipal Police Services are trained in mental resiliency in the face of trauma. As both a military police officer and a civilian police officer, the training was essential to prepare me and to help me identify individuals in crisis due to trauma. On some of those occasions, I would be compelled to take those individuals into temporary custody in order to get them to a hospital to get the help they needed. I mentioned before that many who suffer from post-traumatic injuries do not realize the extent of the injury they have endured, if they are able to recognize the issue at all. I have many friends who only realized how much they were injured because their families had to step in as part of an intervention, telling their spouses to get help because they see the symptoms being presented which are abnormal and unhealthy. It takes social networks, including family, and connections in the person's professional life to ensure that treatment is received. Stigma still exists in these professions as well, and I have seen it especially so in civilian policing. I blame some of this on the lack of people willing to perform the job of a police officer, and when an officer calls in sick, the workload of that missing person must be split with those who remain on the job that day. The lack of bodies in these workplaces creates a feeling of resentment if someone is off work from these high-tempo careers who are suffering from an invisible injury. I have heard many officers refer to it as "snap leave", meaning that the officer off work simply 'snapped' because they could no longer handle the job. The burnout these officers are facing that have resulted in long-term absence from work is rarely met with compassion. This mentality negatively impacts others around who are still suffering silently and who will then be afraid to take time off work to address their mental health because they don't want to be seen as weak in front of their peers.

Careers where a lack of compassion for their employees' mental health can quickly turn into a poisonous environment. We, as employees, can prevent the workplace from becoming a poisonous environment through rigorous compassion, thoughtful policies, and mental health resources. It takes leadership from both the lowest levels of patrol officers and the highest levels of the executive branch to eliminate the lack of mental health awareness and the stigma against seeking psychological help in the workplace.

Chapter 8
Lack of Support in the Workplace

The workplace, whether it be the military, the police service, the fire department, emergency medical services, or any other business entity, share a main goal: protecting their own interests (at least, that's the way I've perceived it in my time as both a soldier and a police officer). I have found that, in the highest echelons of leadership, there is a percentage of the role that calls for politics, which is generally distasteful for those who have suffered a Post Traumatic Injury. When I was suffering from the Post Traumatic Injury and the multiple emotional issues, and psychological dysregulation, I found myself believing I was speaking candidly to my peers and superiors but, in reality, I was having exaggerated reactions from the extreme and defensive emotions I had at the time. A lack of support in the workplace leads to a lack of morale and an inevitable decrease for an employee with respect to wanting to be present both physically and mentally for the job. The mindset resulting from a lack of support creates a level of insecurity and depression. As a first responder it increases the risk to your life and mental health on the job, not including the wellbeing of, and impact on, your coworkers and family. Ultimately, support in the workplace is the duty of the leadership responsible for it, and if they're not doing their job properly, it becomes a toxic work environment.

Jesse Hewitt

Poor morale and attitude are easily observable and infectious in the workplace, and can be due to ignorance, maliciousness, or lack of insight at the leadership level. A shortfall in leadership results in personnel suffering from mental health issues and can lead to many more egregious issues within the workplace which erodes the members' mental health further and creates contempt against the employer. Some of these issues include making mistakes when normally they wouldn't happen, which happened to me on the job as a cop. One evening after bringing in a young man who I arrested with a prohibited firearm on him (that he used to rob someone), I left the police station and ended up running two red light intersections with cameras before the end of my shift. It was brought to my attention by my boss, and I had absolutely no recollection of having done so, a mistake I had never done in my career up to that point. Mistakes and distractions while attempting to do the job of a first responders puts everyone's wellbeing, and even lives, at risk.

When I left the army in 2018, I was burned out and had given a lot of myself in sacrificing my body, as well as my emotional and psychological wellbeing, in service to my country. I thought that by leaving the army my psychological and physical symptoms of PTSD would go away, and I could leave that experience behind me. Unfortunately, this ignorance would turn around to bite me years later. I had stopped seeing a mental health professional the moment I was hired by the police service until my diagnosis in late 2019 – to the detriment of my health. The interruption on my road to better mental health set me back and made the climb harder to get back to where I was with regards to a healthy mental mindset. I did eventually get the psychological treatment that helped me recover to a point where I was healthier than ever before, but the initial decision to stop treatment when I started a new career as a police officer definitely delayed that progress.

There were moments in both my policing and military careers where the lack of support in the workplace was noticeable in both a professional sense, and with regards to mental health recognition. I was making errors in judgement on the job that brought scrutiny from my bosses down upon me. I talked to them candidly about my mental health struggles and disclosed that I was seeing a psychologist again; unfortunately, there is a stigma about mental health in policing, and it was common for me to hear gossip amongst my peers about other officers' mental health. They frequently called it "snap leave" (As in, the cop finally "snapped") whenever an officer had to take time off work to address their psychological and emotional struggles. I'm of the opinion that the military has much better recognition of mental health injuries and encourages members to seek mental health assistance both during and post career, severely outweighing the level of support I received with the police service. The end of my policing career happened due to my own resignation, when I found out that the service had deemed that my mental health injury posed 'undue hardship' on them, and they had hired their own 'mental health professional' to go through my PTSD diagnosis report and claim that I was unable to work as a police officer any longer. I was so disgusted by this revelation that I contacted my Veterans Affairs office and got set up with the Rehabilitation and Vocational Assistance program which enabled me to leave the policing world behind me. I had recognized by that point, through therapy, that leaving the military to pursue policing was simply increasing my risk of relapse with regards to the psychological injuries. Each shift had a chance to expose me to a circumstance that would cause a relapse in my symptoms, and there had already been several events that caused a relapse by the time I decided to leave the first responder lifestyle behind. I could, and did, heal from the PTSI's (depression, suicidal ideation, alcohol abuse, etc.), but working in the field of work of policing put me at risk of experiencing a scenario that could trigger a relapse in symptoms. I firmly believe, to this day, that the best option for me was to remove myself from the role of a first responder and focus on a career that supported first responders instead. In my opinion, which continues to this day, years after I departed the career of a first responder, leaving an environment that could elicit more trauma or triggering incidents from previous trauma was not going to help me in my long-term recovery. It is a high-risk, high-reward environment, and there is a reason many first responder careers tend to be close knit and don't associate with other 'civilians'. They don't understand the dark humor involved in those careers, nor the trauma that people in each of those professions are exposed to on the daily. I needed to remove myself from that environment for my own betterment. By doing so, I removed myself from a position where the lack of support from the workplace could injure me further, and I could now focus on my own best interests related to my mental health going forward.

Lack of support in the workplace can initially appear inconsequential. Seemingly insignificant slights at first. Those insignificant slights against us are usually not personal attacks on our character from a superior, and are very likely not directed at you nor I. It's rather our actions (which should be recognized), are part of an oversight on behalf of the employer. They're not seeing how much we're suffering nor the effort we put in to get the job done. In one instance, a little over a year after I returned from an operational tour in Libya, I was informed that I would be getting a commendation from the army. I was proud of myself, although we as Canadians and soldiers were expected to remain humble. I felt that we, as a team, deserved proper recognition for being able to accomplish the evacuation of an embassy in the middle of a civil war without suffering any casualties. The day came and a friend of mine who was on tour with me was nominated for a commendation as well. This ceremony wasn't just for the two of us. Several other soldiers had been nominated for various levels of commendations from the military for diverse reasons. The different levels of commendations were awarded to each recipient, and they were called in groups to get their commendations together, with a speech read out for the reasons behind each commendation. I was called up with another soldier and we both received our commendations. Mine was issued first on a plaque and my picture was taken. A speech was given by the officer presenting it, explaining why I was being presented the commendation which included a powerful speech about the conflict in Libya and the team's extraordinary performance of tasks when evacuating civilian personnel from the embassy. As I marched off, the next person, haven been given the <u>same</u> commendation, was presented their award. The speech introducing this soldier explained that they were being presented with the same level of

Post-Traumatic Growth

commendation because they organized a unit barbeque in order to increase unit morale a couple months earlier, in Canada. I was stunned by what I was witnessing at the time. It took away the significance of the commendation for me. I felt that the impact of what I had accomplished with the taskforce I worked with overseas was minimized by the presentation of the same commendation to two extremely different scenarios. It was disheartening, and what I expected to be a large accomplishment in my professional career was demoted to a plaque I threw in my desk at home. Sometimes exceptional service without proper recognition can deeply injure a person, especially when that service comes at such a personal cost, such as psychological or physical injuries.

I noticed that these slights were grating on my mind and body, and I needed a change. I also noticed that the lack of support in the workplace as a police officer, and the role and duties I had in the policing career, were putting me at risk of relapse and psychological injuries again. It was, and remains, my belief that in my circumstances, with the psychological injuries I had already suffered in the past, I wouldn't be able to recover as quickly. I felt that I was inadvertently increasing my chance at further injuring myself prior to being fully recovered. I won't say that this is the case for everyone, because I know plenty of first responders who were injured and recovered without a change in career, but I felt a change was necessary for me. Once I decided to leave the field of policing, it felt as if a great weight was lifted off my body. I reflect now on my accomplishments as both a soldier and a police officer and I have great pride in what I've accomplished and the lives I've had a positive impact on. It took me a while to figure out that my accomplishments were not because of my career, which I used to define myself, but because of my individual actions as a person acting in the role of a soldier or police officer. Some careers attract a certain mindset of the public, and I don't think it's a stretch to assume that people interested in a career as a first responder do so because they want to help people more than anything else.

Every accomplishment or mistake I made in my personal or professional life weren't because of my career, but because of my personal mindset and actions. I've seen other people blame their poor decisions on their jobs, psychological injuries, etc. At the end of the day, psychological injuries or not, a person is responsible for their actions. By removing myself from the titles, uniforms, and badges, I was able to come to terms with myself and move on to something new that didn't expose me, every shift, to blood, carnage, or violence. Once I removed myself from first responder environment and mindset, my recovery escalated exponentially. A change of scenery was what I needed to help jump start my recovery, and I'm glad I did it because I realize now that I'm healthier for it.

Chapter 9
A New Perspective on Old Ways

It is important to utilize the most effective tools for the specific tasks they were designed for. For example, you would use a chainsaw to log up a tree trunk, not a fork. In the army and in policing, there are similar training methods with regards to assessing situations. Some of that training is also taught in corporate business (Ryder and Downs, 2022). The importance of ensuring that you are constantly acquiring new tools for your mental toolbox. When I speak about the mental toolbox, I'm referring to easily retrievable information that you can consciously access. The mental toolbox can be something like memorizing all the moves in chess in order to become a more proficient player. In order to become more resilient to psychological trauma, it's important to fill your mental toolbox with productive and protective measures that focus on increasing your skillset in order to manage intrusive symptoms associated with trauma. Becoming complacent will lead to mental stagnation and prevents you from growing, progressing successfully, as well as experiencing recovery. I believe that some of the tools previously learned through first responder careers can be re-utilized to assist in both mental health recovery and, eventually, not only ensuring psychological resilience, but what I refer to as Post Traumatic Growth.

I have learned that, although resilience is admirable, growth is the ultimate objective when dealing with a diagnosis of PTSD. Post Traumatic Growth (PTG) is the positive psychological changes that emerge following a traumatic event. Greater and new appreciation for life, learning about personal strength, even spiritual growth and strengthening relationships with others, are possible. I know this because I achieved those all personally.

While on a Close Quarters Battle course in the military, concepts were taught in order to assist us in having the most optimal advantage over our adversaries as possible. Various theories were taught to us and those concepts were utilized to enhance the chance of success for each member of the team and to ensure we acted in a connected and fluid motion. 'Flooding' a room to ensure full coverage of every nook and cranny was covered by the team. Working together silently, swiftly and carefully to achieve full domination of the dwelling that they're 'clearing'. Theories such as the OODA Loop (observe, orient, decide, act) and Hicks Law all help a team achieve their joint objective through superior speed, surprise, flexibility, coordination, and communication. Of those theories, I believe at least two can be used in order to help ensure proactive resilience against negative stimulus and hopefully manage positive psychological growth.

Hicks Law, as well as several other theories used in military/paramilitary first responder careers, are also practiced in top tier sports leagues. Created by two psychologists, William Hick and Ray Hyman, the concept was first drafted in 1952 in an experimental psychology paper "On the Rate of Gain of Information" (Proctor et al., 2004). The work within that paper eventually became known as Hicks Law and focused on the study of human information processing. To break it down more simply, the theory breaks down the idea that the more options a person has to solve a problem, the longer until that person acts upon it (Hyman, 1953). For example, for a fire fighter responding to a building fire, they must quickly assess the situation, determine the best course of action, and communicate this information to their team. It's extremely important that the fire fighters are trained in what method is the quickest and safest way to prioritize and extinguish the fire. Clear, concise protocols ensure that the decision-making time is shortened in order to speed up the reaction time. Another example is with military operations. In such operations, quick and effective decision making can determine a mission's success or failure. In the heat of a battle, the commanding officer must quickly assess the situation, determine the best course of action, and communicate those orders to their platoon. Taking Hicks Law into consideration, the more alternatives the commanding officer issues means the reaction time of the platoon will take longer. The commanding officer, well-trained in battle theory and situational awareness, will instead provide clear and concise operational plans in order to guide the platoon to quick and decisive actions.

Sayings you may have heard before (it was common vernacular during my time in the military), such as "Keep it Simple, Stupid!" are delved directly from the core concepts of Hicks Law. The less options you have available to you to tackle a problem, the quicker your reaction time will be. Hick proposed that the relationship between the reaction time and the number of choices available to a person could be measured logarithmically (which is a fancy way of saying there is a way to see the relationship between two variables). Hyman managed an experiment which determined a linear relation between reaction time and the information transmitted (Hyman, 1953). After reading the last few sentences I have written, you may be thinking to yourself "This doesn't seem like Keeping it Simple Stupid..." but it really is so please, bear with me.

In his original study, Hick showed that reaction time increased as the number of response options also increased (Hick, 1952). A person with two options to respond to a stimulus (for example: two coins on a table) reacted within the range of 0.2-0.3 seconds whereas a person with four options (four coins) had a response time that was over 0.4 seconds, six choices (six coins) was over 0.5 seconds, and so on (Hicks 1952).

The reaction time is lengthened not only by the *number* of options, but also the *compatibility* of the response to the stimulus. To make it simple, the more you're familiar with an object, the faster you can react to it. This has been labelled as the "Stimulus-Response Compatibility" (Kornblum et al., 1990). It showed that the type of responses (how we react) we have to address the stimuli are directly related to how fast we can react to the stimuli. The reaction time can be further shortened with training for specific circumstances, assuming stereotypes, and prior knowledge.

A 'Kill House' is a term used by military and law enforcement to describe a training facility used to conduct close-quarters combat (CQC), also known as close-quarters battle (CQB) and room clearing exercise. It is typically a house built within a larger facility, with hallways, doors, windows, and multiple stories with stairs. The purpose is to provide as close to real life training and scenarios in a controlled environment as possible. Live fire and non-live fire scenarios can be completed in the kill house, and it allows personnel to develop the skills and confidence needed to effectively operate in a CQC environment. Stimulus within the kill house can be trained actors, or targets if it's a live-fire scenario. Kill houses are a very important aspect of military and law enforcement training, as well as fire and emergency services. Simulated stress helps train and prepare these professionals for the real-life impact and quick decision making required to succeed and save lives. What this science means in a CQC environment is that: with the right training and tools for the stimuli in the kill house, the faster the reaction time is to the stimulus. Additionally, having the right tools available to address that stimulus also shortens the reaction time. For example, unless you're John Wick walking through the first door of the kill house armed with a pencil and a carbine against an armed assailant, your response choice to that level of threat will be the carbine over the pencil. The reaction time will be faster in this scenario due to the lack of compatibility of a pencil versus an armed threat against the greater compatibility of the carbine, because it isn't the correct instrument for that objective. What it boils down to is having the right tool for the job.

Everyone practices Hicks Law throughout their lives. There is rarely only one option to use as a reaction to a stimulus or scenario that requires problem-solving. As a practice in CQB and other combative scenarios, the training encourages the most advantageous option to overcome the opponent every single time.

Hicks Law was initially taught to me while I was in the military, and I was introduced to it a second time during Use of Force training at the Ontario Police College. Every officer in the province of Ontario must attend Ontario Police College prior to being deployed in whichever city they were hired. Hicks Law concepts were the same and were usually taught side-by-side with the concepts of muscle memory (muscle memory being the concept that practicing a single action over and over, hundreds, if not thousands of times, will lead to the automatic response of the action).

The OODA Loop

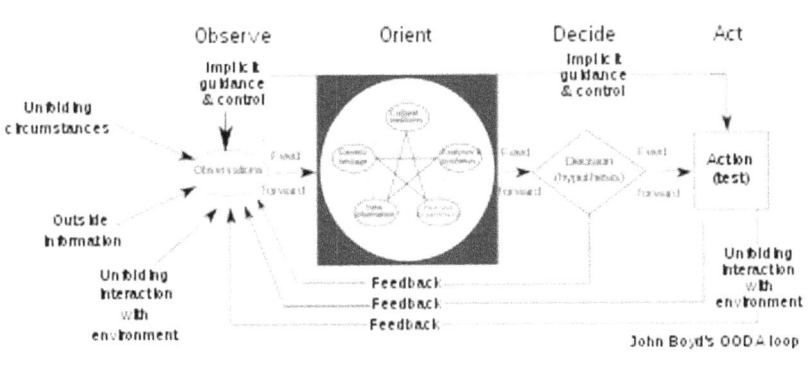

(Richards, 2012)

The second theory previously mentioned was the OODA Loop. The OODA Loop stands for Observe, Orient, Decide and Act. Created by Colonel John Boyd of the USAF, a former fighter pilot who applied the concept to superiority in combat. His goal at the time, not realizing how encompassing the theory would become, was to figure out what made the most proficient fighter pilot dogfighter. The picture above appears complicated, and it may be unfamiliar to some readers that are not first responders.

The first of the four steps is to Observe. This step includes person looking at (observing) the situation unfolding with the purpose of building the most accurate and encompassing picture (Boyd, 1987). To do so, the observer is collecting as much information, from as many sources as are available, to observe. I'll provide a real-life example of how I utilized the OODA loop and how it's broken down. Firstly, I will address the *Observe* step.

Post-Traumatic Growth

Personal Anecdote
Trigger Warning – Discusses Suicide, Crime Scene Imagery
This passage interchanges between the <u>narrative</u> content and the <u>personal anecdote</u> content.
You will find a "END OF PASSAGE" notice to indicate where narrative content continues <u>without</u> referencing the <u>personal anecdote</u>.

One evening while on a policing shift, I was parked outside of a restaurant compiling notes when a silver pickup truck parked beside me. A man exited the driver's seat and began walking towards my driver's side door. I exited my vehicle to meet him and to ask him what he needed. He appeared distressed and worried, and quickly began telling me that he had a female friend in his truck and that he believed her abusive ex-husband had broken into her house. The man explained that he was a friend of the female and had been picking her up at the end of her shift to drop her off at her house at night, and that when they arrived this evening, they saw the bloody note on the front door. He explained that the police service I was working for had arrested the man two weeks earlier for being physically violent with her, and that he had strict conditions to stay away from the residence, as well as to refrain from contacting her through any medium.

The ex-husband had apparently phoned the hydro utilities and had the electricity shut off to the house, leaving it in complete darkness until it could be reconnected. I asked the man why he thought the ex-husband had broken inside the house and he said the front door had a bloody letter at its doorstep outside the house when he tried to drop off his friend at her house, and, that around the back of the house, the basement window had been smashed in. I was informed that the moment they saw the broken window and the bloody note, they got back in his pickup and were on the way to the police station when they saw me and decided to report to me instead. I walked over to the female who was sitting in the passenger seat of the pickup and opened her door. She was weeping heavily, holding the paper in her hands. It was a standard piece of lined paper you would see in any notebook. It was so saturated in blood that it had no white left on it. It was barely keeping itself from falling apart and had to be cradled from underneath to hold its form flat. I was told that they thought the blood was the ex-husband's. I quickly scanned the note and was convinced that the man was likely hoping she would enter the home so he could kill her and then himself. The blood on the paper I, too, assumed was the ex-husband's.

All the information I received at this point of the investigation was with relation to the *Observe* portion of the OODA loop. I was not categorizing the information, because I needed to understand the full picture of what was going on before I could orient myself to the situation properly and, as a result, plan accordingly. As I received as much information as possible, I then phoned my on-duty Sergeant and gave him the information I had been given thus far. Given the severity of the possible outcomes inside that residence we needed to act quickly, understanding that the risk of grievous bodily harm or death was a real possibility. I was told to meet him, and several other officers, at the exterior of the residence to orient ourselves to the situation before going in. I needed to begin the 'Orient' portion of the OODA loop now, ensuring that I wasn't missing any information and to best utilize the information I had to ensure the safety of the public and deal with whatever person(s) that may remain inside the house.

I told the male and female to go to a friend's house nearby to await further communication from police. The female provided me with a key to the front door of the house and I took the suicide note from her. I drove to the street where the house was located and met up with my Sergeant and several other officers. We checked the front door, seeing blood drops on it and on the front porch. The interior of the house was dark due to the power outage by the hydro company on behalf of the ex-husband, and we confirmed that, at the rear of the house, the basement window was smashed.

At this point in time, the *Orientation* portion of the OODA Loop is being utilized. We have gathered all available information and now we need to filter it, analyze what is and is not important, assess the potential threats, opportunities, routes of entries, and ensure that we have all

Post-Traumatic Growth

the resources necessary to handle the situation and proceed to appropriately tackle the objective. The actions to be taken would ensure as high a chance of success as possible combined with the smallest margin of error. Now that I had observed and oriented myself to the objective, the next step was to use all the information I had at my disposal and decide what to do with it. I needed to decide before I could act.

We oriented ourselves to the object: A detached house, potential subject (who could also be a victim due to, likely, self-inflicted blood loss), unknown weapons, a subject with a history of violence inside the house in an unknown location, point of entry at back of the house, a house with multiple floors, and lack of power inside the house. That meant, at a minimum, we were operating at a disadvantage and had to use flashlights in our off-hands (non-dominant hands) while holding service pistols in our main hands (dominant hand). This meant less accuracy combined with poor vision inside an unfamiliar environment. We had no reason to obtain a warrant to enter the household and we had a key to get in the front door because we had permission from one of the owners to enter. We had reason to believe the ex-husband was at least bleeding, and was likely planning a murder/suicide. He had no known access to firearms, confirmed by his ex-wife, and established that the only weapons inside were the knives in the kitchen.

The incoming stream of information we were receiving had culminated to a point where we had oriented ourselves to the situation, and now we needed to move on to the next portion of the OODA Loop, *Decide*. We had compiled the raw information into something that we could action as a single cohesive unit. Each of us had a basic level of training provided by the police college, with some of us having advanced training or experience that transcended police training, as was the case with my own military training. This ensured that when we went into the house, as part of a 'stack' (group) of officers working together, the level of training that the police service had us familiar with set us up to know how each officer would operate and react inside. Training in First-Aid, room clearing, and use of force is all re-qualified once per year, in a one, or two-day period. That means that of the approximately 2000 working hours in a calendar year, about 36 hours is training in First-Aid, high-threat room clearing, firearms training and use of force. That is a dreadfully low number of training hours for a job where the officers', and the public's, lives are on the line each day. We knew the outcome of inaction would likely be the death of the ex-husband inside. We were all equipped with flashlights to deal with the darkness inside, enabling us to enter. We decided that going through the front door with the key was better than trying to get through the basement window, or breaching through another window on the main level. We predicted that the man inside was either bleeding out (or had intensions too), and we needed to act appropriately to stop that from happening. Given the threat level of the situation, our safest option for action was to enter as multiple officers in a 'stack' on entry, and maintaining that 'stack' within the residence while conducting methodical clearing of the main and upper floor.

After we *Decide* our plan of action, we need to test the hypothesis of the plan-of-action through the final portion of the OODA Loop, *Act*. After gathering and compiling all available information, determining what the best course of action will be (with that information in mind), and forming it into a hypothesis as the best course of action to respond with, we now executed the hypothesis to determine the outcome.

I had the key to the front door and I put it in the keyhole. Another officer held his gun on the front of the door as I opened it and we began the slow 'flood' (like a river of water flowing into the room) of the 'stack' of officers into the residence. Upon entry, we called out the man's name, announced that the police were inside the residence and that he wasn't to move but instead to call out to us. We received nothing but silence. When I entered the residence, the walls of the hallways had large blood smears on them, as if a large man had cut both his wrists and walked up the hall, smearing his bloody arms all along the walls as he moved, intended as a message to his ex-wife. The flashlights we held illuminated the hallway; casting shadows that made the hall appear much longer than it should have. As the 'stack' cleared into the hallway, we made it to the kitchen on the main floor. I saw that the kitchen table had blood smeared all over it; the kitchen walls were also blood-smeared. The amount of blood loss at this point was significant

Post-Traumatic Growth

enough to cement the idea into my mind that the person bleeding would need emergency medical assistance. I called out again, announcing that police were inside, and I heard a male voice moan from the second story up the stairs, opposite of the kitchen hallway. The other officers with me heard it as well and I led the 'stack' up the stairs.

The same, heavy smear of blood ran up the walls of the stairs. We used the flashlights in our hands to illuminate around the corners of the stairwell and railings as much as possible. I did not want to get ambushed from above, so I attempted to see as much as I could. As I got to the top of the stairs, I saw four closed doors in front of me. A small, five-by-five carpeted area was in front of me, and I saw a door to the left, two doors directly ahead of me and a final door on my right. All of them held the 'unknown' inside, meaning I did not have any information to determine what was behind any of those doors. All had an equal chance of having a bloody subject behind it.

The OODA Loop is cyclical in nature. What I mean by that is: it rotates back around to the beginning phase the moment it is finished. The loop is constantly in motion, and the moment the *Act* happens, you have the opportunity to begin *Observing* the new information available to you after engaging in the hypothesis. The future loop will be more accurate, allowing a more streamlined (i.e., faster!) OODA loop as the objective becomes narrower and more familiar.

Jesse Hewitt

TRIGGER WARNING - CRIME SCENE DETAILS

As I was at the top of the stairs, I heard a male moan, seemingly of pain, coming from the door immediately to my right. I turned and held my gun and flashlight focused on the corner of the door that went into the room. With my partner officers at my back, I palmed the doorknob, feeling that it was unlocked. I held my flashlight in my left hand, allowing me enough dexterity to twist the doorknob with my palm while my pistol was trained on the door. My OODA Loop now engaged again. I had observed that the lone male subject was very likely behind the door, oriented myself to the door to ensure I could act as fast as the door opened in the slightest.

As the door opened, I could see dim light coming from inside. The light was coming from several candles laid on the tiled floor of what I found was a bathroom. The candles were atop the lid of the closed toilet, the counter, and the floor. Near the candles were framed pictures of the female I had seen earlier, weeping and holding a blood covered note in her hands. The bathtub was full of blood-red water, and blood was smeared on the floor, walls, and bathroom sink mirror. The low ambient light provided by the candles made the scene appear like something out of a horror movie. The moaning I had heard was coming from a large naked man in the bathtub. His right arm was slit from the base of his inner wrist in a straight line to his inner elbow. He rested this arm with his palm up on the ledge of the bathtub. His left arm was submerged in the bloody bathtub he was half concealed within.

I saw, beside one of the candles, a retractable 'exacto' knife, bloodied with the blade still open. I called out to the man and told him not to move. I warned him that if he moved and reached for that knife, I would shoot him. He was motionless prior to me speaking and I wondered for a fraction of a second if he had died with the last moan I heard. I considered that it could have been the air escaping from his dead lungs.

After that fraction of a second had passed, and I had finished calling out my warning, he started moving. He raised his left arm from the water, showing me that he had also attempted to cut his left wrist.

Post-Traumatic Growth

He'd done a poor job, only managing several superficial cuts. It appeared to me that he had cut his right wrist first, but by doing so, he'd damaged the tendons to a point where he couldn't handle the knife in his right hand well enough to manage a deep cut on his left arm.

He did not move, so I grabbed the knife and threw it away from his reach. I ordered him to stand up but he was barely able to respond. I now saw, beside the tub, that there were several empty bottles of wine. There were also bottles of pain medication, such as Advil and Tylenol, spilled over the counter. I assumed he was taking them to thin his blood so he would bleed out faster. When he moved, his semi-clotted, mangled right arm opened back up and began bleeding freely again.

I reached in, grabbed him, and dragged his naked body violently out of the tub. I did not stop until I got him onto the carpeted upper stair foyer. With other officers helping hold him, I put a tourniquet on his arm and tied it tight until he cried out. I felt no sympathy for him. He had beat his spouse only weeks earlier and, in my opinion, would have killed her if she had come inside the house instead of me and my partners. We called downstairs as the paramedics had arrived and were waiting for us to give the 'all-clear' to come into the house. We assisted the paramedics and carried him out to the ambulance where he was arrested for break and enter, violating the terms of his release, and a slew of other disgusting offences.

END OF PASSAGE

The OODA Loop and Hicks Law training I received prior to this situation helped prepare me, as well as my partners, that evening. We entered a dynamic and extreme situation, which was dealt with quickly and without physical consequence to any of us. The conceptual training that allowed us to break down how we approach stressful events, with the drive and determination to succeed, while keeping the training as straight forward as possible kept us alive. I believe that a large amount of training we receive throughout our lives can be utilized on a personal level. Using any form of training to make ourselves wiser to our surroundings, rather than simply tackling obstacles in front of us blindly, helps us be successful. The more training we receive, the more well-rounded in our thought process we become. Whether it's personal experiences leading to wisdom, or professional training we can use to further personal agendas outside of a workplace setting, all skills obtained through training and life lessons should be utilized as part of our mental toolbox of resources.

A familiar example would be that a child utilizes a form of the OODA Loop when he or she plays catch with their parent. When the ball is coming toward them, they observe the trajectory of the ball, then orient themselves to assume where it is going and decide if they can catch it. They can include personal experience and knowledge they have gained from playing this game of catch in the past to help them assess their course of action. The child then decides how, or if, they will catch the ball. Finally, the child acts upon it. If the child fails to catch the ball, they'll try a different approach next time. If the child catches the ball, the OODA Loop resets and the child now has to determine what to do next: keep the ball, throw it, or something else entirely.

What I am saying is that, everyone uses these skills to a varying degree. It is part of who we are as people, and our experiences determine how effective we are with those skills in our daily lives. Understanding the core concepts within them, however, allow us to be conscious of how important the concepts are. I believe that these skills, built through understanding and reutilizing the theories of Hicks Law and the OODA Loop, can be used to assist with handling the onset of mental health trauma symptoms. They are tools for our mental health toolbox, assisting us in understanding what is going on around us and reacting to it safely and quickly.

One of the things taught to me when suffering panic and anxiety attacks was to focus on breathing. Deep, long breaths (ex. taking a deep relaxing breath before entering into a hostile environment) help calm your mind and prepare you for the event that is to unfold, as well as during the experience. If I feel the tremor of an anxiety attack building up inside of me, I focus on that feeling, taking it in, and consciously thinking about how it's affecting me. I take in all the information happening around me so I can determine the cause of the anxiety, and I focus on it. I acknowledge the feelings of stress: increased heartrate, perspiration, and shaking hands. I need to trust that my body is sensing stimulus that is triggering anxiety, whether that feeling is justified or not, I know it's a real experience for me. As I'm focusing on the feelings of anxiety and stress, I breathe deeply, and begin calming myself before it has a chance to overwhelm me. I begin orienting myself to the information I can obtain given the circumstances that have likely caused some level of tunnel vision. If my anxiety has me crippled to a point that I can barely function, I find a spot to sit down and avoid external stimuli in order to address the internal issues I'm suffering from in the moment. As I am oriented, I assess what, if any, of my surroundings may be triggering the anxiety attack. Once I've looked around my surroundings, taken several deep breaths, I then decide what I think it's going to take to reduce the chances of me having a 'full-on' anxiety or panic attack. Do I have access to medication that will help address the symptoms? Have I recognized that I can remove myself from the negative stimulus that's triggering the symptoms? Once I've decided the best course of action, I take it. If the act of removing myself from the situation, or taking the medication, helps alleviate the anxiety or panic from continuing to build in my body, then my OODA Loop resets so I can maintain that recovery of calming myself down to a neutral point. If the act I've decided upon doesn't work, then my OODA Loop resets and I begin looking at other options that may better address the symptoms while continuously practicing the breathing techniques. This gives me a chance to reassess another avenue that will reduce anxiety or panic. Even if nothing works, and a 'full-blown' anxiety or panic attack happens, that doesn't mean I'm a failure. What it gives me is experience for the next time I'm in a similar situation. It gives me the knowledge that something happened in that moment, and it allows me the opportunity to talk to a professional whom would, hopefully, better interpret what, in that moment, may have triggered the issues that wreaked havoc on my mind and body.

It's important to remember that, while I'm talking about these concepts as if they're easy and a simple transition, it isn't. It takes time and effort to learn to transfer these skills and use them to protect my mental health from an anxiety attack, panic attack, or other emotional reaction. These skills, having already been learned and used to protect our physical selves while serving our country, can then be used outside of our careers and used for ourselves (whether those be Hicks Law, the OODA Loop, or other coping mechanisms).

Post Traumatic Stress Injuries are both a psychological injury and a physical brain injury. To fail at attempting to utilize a philosophical theory of combat under stress of a physical brain injury is not a sign of weakness. It takes time to get better, similarly to a badly broken ankle that requires physiotherapy after it heals. When I speak to others, I regularly compare mental health recovery to physiotherapy, because if you stop going to physiotherapy for a twisted ankle just because it's not sore after the first session, that pain will come back. You can't quit therapy, physical or emotional, cold turkey. The symptoms will come back, which means that dedication to getting better, even after some of the symptoms subside, is paramount. It takes patience, and it takes losing sometimes to gain the ability to recognize your limitations before you're able to stand on two feet psychologically.

One of the most impactful messages I learned in my readings throughout recovery was *"Don't blame yourself if you relapse,"* when I was tackling my most personal, and at the time what I considered my most shameful, injury: bulimia. It's okay to fail at a task that requires an injured brain to succeed, and it's okay to fail when learning a new

Post-Traumatic Growth

skill in general. Even with professionals, success is not going to happen one-hundred-percent of the time. Mistakes happen, and until those mistakes occur, a person's fortitude is not properly measured. Many first responders that have suffered from a PTSI whom I know personally, myself included, are extremely hard on themselves upon failing an objective that they feel is important. It took me reading it and hearing it and finally experiencing failure and picking myself up again in order to learn from my peers and professionals that relapsing (what I once considered failing) at a mental health recovery effort isn't the end of the world. It's okay to relapse sometimes, because it's part of the effort to heal. It's okay not to be perfect, and it's okay to get up off the ground and keep fighting.

Strength isn't determined by how fast a person overcomes an obstacle, but rather how many times they pick themselves up during the journey. It's also called perseverance, accepting failure and learning to get back up and learn from that loss in order to succeed next time. Perseverance and failure go hand-in-hand, but so do learning and success. Delayed success is still success.

In summary, using tools learned throughout your career (Hicks Law, OODA Loop, exposure therapy, the road to mental readiness) can be harnessed and refocused to help handle mental health trauma. It's incredibly difficult to learn new skills while suffering from a psychological injury. In order to help acknowledge that, I reutilized previously learned skills and tethered them to assist my psychological process to protect my mind and body instead of using it as it was taught to me – a manner with which to overwhelm an enemy. It took me a while to understand that a mental health injury does not make an enemy of yourself. I needed to respect the injury for what it was, instead of trying to attack it as if it were a foe.

Chapter 10
Muscle Memory & Physical Health

I mentioned in the last chapter the difficulty of learning new skills while suffering from a psychological injury. A PTSI that has resulted in high levels of anxiety, depression, sleep disorders, or substance abuse can cause severe issues in memory and attention. The long-term stress associated with having psychological injuries (PTSD for example) can damage portions of the brain, specifically the hippocampus (Apfel et al., 2011). The hippocampus is a part of the human brain and is most associated with memory consolidation and decision making, both of which are affected detrimentally when an individual suffers from PTSD (Apfel et al., 2011). Several studies have been conducted on samples of PTSD in combat veterans showing hippocampal atrophy in conjunction with decreased function in memory retention and memory forming. All that jargon is to say that an injured veteran's brain actually shrinks in response to the overwhelming stress (Apfel et al., 2011). The hippocampus controls learning and memory, and has been shown to change (shrink) in response to trauma.

Chronic stress, traumatic brain injuries (TBIs), and other psychiatric disorders in veterans and other first responders can be measured through psychological testing and mapping of the brain. A study conducted on veterans who have current, chronic PTSD, and veterans who have recovered from PTSD, showed a six percent shrinkage in those who were currently suffering (Apfel et al., 2011). It turns out the 'invisible' injury of having chronic PTSD in veterans has the physical effect of shrinking that portion of the brain which allows humans to learn, regulate emotions and both form and retrieve memories. Fortunately, damage to the hippocampus is not permanent, provided the injury is treated appropriately. (Smith, 2005)

One of the more frustrating issues I suffer from, especially during those painful years prior to diagnosis, is my short-term memory function. I found, and still find, myself forgetting the simple tasks that I would normally never have an issue with. It started with small simple things, like forgetting a couple items at the grocery store, or forgetting the list entirely at home. As my other symptoms worsened with the PTSI, my memory worsened as well. I started having to keep post-its around the house to make sure I could tackle simple chores, making lists on my phone with daily alarms so I didn't forget anything important. I found myself forgetting appointments, birthdays, to do the laundry, etc. I would easily get distracted and I found it difficult to learn new things because I had become so inflexible in my mindset. It got so bad that it became difficult to take in multiple pieces of information at once. I would not be able to have background noise, like the TV playing, and simultaneously have a conversation with someone. My mind couldn't focus on one or the other while they were both happening at once, making it impossible for me to concentrate on either. Sometimes I would stare off into the distance or through objects until someone snapped me out of it.

Although damage to the hippocampus can explain the symptoms of memory loss, memory organization, other symptoms that regularly occur while suffering from a PTSI, are usually present as well (Samuelson, 2011). Whether it is dissociation, flashbacks, depression, suicidal/homicidal behaviour, or behavioural issues, veterans or first responders suffering from complex PTSD have the arduous task of treating not one symptom, but likely half a dozen or more. It is a massive undertaking for anyone, so you can imagine how it could feel near impossible to accomplish for someone suffering from a PTSI without outside assistance.

Some injuries of the brain can be treated with medication. When people experience stress, the body releases cortisol – a hormone that controls mood, fear, and stress. It is related to the 'fight or flight' response we have and can be regulated through medication like Prozac. I cannot speak for the efficiency of anti-depressants, or other psychotropic medication because I'm neither a doctor, nor do I have any personal experience with them. I would expect that anyone who has seen a mental health professional and was prescribed medication, to take it as directed.

Suffering from memory loss and a hindered ability to learn new skills created the necessity for me to rely on previous training, instead of, what felt like, a frustratingly futile attempt at learning new skills. New skills that I was being taught in the police academy after leaving the army were difficult to retain. I found myself getting severe headaches and struggling in contrast to my peers at the time. I explained earlier that utilizing previously learned skills to form a new healthy perspective is a good method of putting some old tools into new use to assist with mental health.

Utilizing previously learned skills as a method of coping and addressing psychological injuries can be beneficial, but it's important to talk with your psychologist about their perspective on that strategy. Post Traumatic Stress Injuries (PTSIs) are fickle things and are so intimately connected with our psyche that they could nearly be described as sentient. They care about you only enough to remain a constant burden and cancerous in nature for your mind. PTSIs have a tendency to interfere with the mental process of the person suffering, pushing them into thinking that the method they're using (alcohol and drug abuse, retreating into gaming, binge eating, etc.) is a healthy process to take their mind of their pain.

The effects of the injury make it easy to suffer for an extended period of time without being cognizant of it. This can lead, as was in my case, to the adoption of poor coping techniques in an effort to reduce the signs of the injury, sometimes without knowing what you're even coping for. Those poor coping techniques are usually harmful to our well-being, and can include drug use, binge drinking, refusal to leave the house, poor diet, no exercise, etc. Efforts to reduce stress, depression, intrusive thoughts, suicidal ideations, and other symptoms can be setback by using negative coping mechanisms such as alcohol, drugs, extreme avoidance behaviours, high-risk behaviours, and more.

When I was suffering prior to diagnosis, and before I chose to acknowledge and accept my injury, I had begun to abuse alcohol as a way to combat the negative effects of the PTSIs I was suffering from. I did not consciously realize that I was using a method of coping that could add further strain onto my life. It was only giving a temporary, brief relief and solution to the issues I was suffering from. That method of coping was not actually confronting the injury, rather helping me hide from it. I was dulling the pain without any long-term plan or goals in mind to combat the injury itself. I didn't have the tools I required to address the injury and begin my recovery. Some of the tools I possessed at the time I had yet to restructure into techniques that would become beneficial to my mental health. I hadn't been able to adapt previously learned training, and at the time, around 2016, I was suffering significantly from memory loss and the inability to learn new skills. Because I didn't have any other skills to rely on, or the self-awareness to seek help, I ended up turning my alcohol consumption into a crutch that I used to combat the symptoms.

I realized later that I had created my own Training Scar by training myself to drink whenever I hurt or felt off, which was most of the time. Training scars are psychological changes that occur after repeated exposure to a specific circumstance. For example, if all I've ever done is open doors outwards, and suddenly I'm faced with a door that opens inward, I'll struggle momentarily and probably push on it before trying to pull it properly. This is because my entire life up to that point has revolved around a specific action (pushing open the door). I had gotten to a point where my conditioned response to stress and anxiety was to drink until I felt better. This action had no basis in reality because alcohol is actually a depressant and was exacerbating my symptoms instead of helping dull them.

Jesse Hewitt

Part of my injury created a deep, seething anger within me; I was burning out and suffering psychologically. I was angry at the world and I felt like I was constantly being treated unfairly. I felt like I was giving everything I had to my job and I wasn't getting enough in return to feel like I was doing something valuable and appreciated. I had a short fuse in both my personal and professional life and, when I did get upset, it would sometimes take me hours, if not days to calm down. That deep anger prevented me from having the willingness to learn when I had already become an instructor in many of the topics, I didn't use the knowledge to help myself at the time because I was refusing to recognize that I had problems. I was stuck acting like it was my way and nothing else and even when I attempted to expand my mindset, I found I was unable to retain the information in my mind or recall it in any structured way – it was coming to me in pieces instead. Lack of memory retention and recall made me extremely upset, and fueled my anger. I began to feel inept and I found myself falling further into depression. The skills I had been utilizing at the time I was suffering were setting me back with regards to my mental health. Although, those skills helped me in the past to overcome obstacles and achieve objectives in my career had resulted in me being stuck in my ways. I had begun to adopt 'Training Scars', which I held onto until I realized that what I was doing was digging myself deeper into despair.

Training Scars are actions that have become habit to the point of muscle memory. Usually, they are lessons learned or taught that have been fast-tracked to achieve a quick solution. They become incredibly hard to drop due to how it becomes so familiar to us and neurologically set within ourselves. The Training Scar may have been beneficial in the past (before it was a scar and was just good training for a specific situation) but it has now become inefficient at best and dangerous at worst. The issue with Training Scars, especially in first responders, is that some of those actions that have been taught and learned over years of operations, is that there is a true likelihood that those actions have saved lives in the past, thus reinforcing the behaviours. For example, for someone to now come up to a me and declare that there is a better way to tackle an objective is very difficult to grasp, especially after

Post-Traumatic Growth

having been using the old method, that's been tested in real life and resulted in saving a life, or succeeding over incredible odds.

Now, sometimes a person's ego can get in the way. With a damaged hippocampus and other psychological injuries such as depression and dissociation, the inability to retain or recall memory and learn new skills may seem like the person is hiding behind an ego, rather than that they simply cannot retain those new skillsets. Those injuries could present themselves to a stranger as an angry, frustrated person. The individual suffering from these injuries may not even consciously accept those injuries yet, whether they've been diagnosed or not. In the high-tempo environment of a first responder it is dangerous to have a lack of personal insight, and in my opinion, a person suffering from a psychological injury related to that field of work must change their role in that profession, even if only temporarily. This would help remove the potential of negative stimulus in order to begin healing, because those stimuli can be inherently triggering to the person that's constantly exposed to dynamic life or death situations.

I usually write each chapter with an explanation of what worked for me to deal with a specific symptom I had, but with regards to Training Scars, I don't have a simple answer or straightforward anecdote to give. I abused substances which allowed me to dull the pain I was suffering from with regards to the depression, memory loss, burnout, lack of support from my ex-wife, and suicidal/homicidal ideation and other negative symptoms associated with the PTSI that I was experiencing. The substance abuse became a daily thing which then turned into a crutch for me. I found myself in my basement most nights of the week, drinking beer or scotch, and I took the opportunity in social gatherings to get drunk. Those were difficult days, and I had to take a long look in the mirror after my diagnosis and determine that I needed help. Nobody can be expected to get better from a psychological injury alone. The African proverb "It takes a village to raise a child" is appropriate for people suffering from a PTSI. As difficult as it was for me to accept that I needed to get better, it was as difficult, if not more-so, to sit down and talk with someone about my injuries. I was forced to relive terrible experiences while also knowing that the information would be recorded. The professional would then be giving me their advice on how to handle myself going forward with the goal to recover and better myself. It's a large obstacle, but succumbing to the 'easy' methods of dulling the pain through drinking and drugs, isn't the answer. Don't become reliant on those methods as a crutch. I had to abstain from drinking for a long time before I was comfortable enough to have a beer without feeling like I was drinking it because I needed to hide from my own mind. It isn't easy – it's not supposed to be. The situations that broke me down were extreme, so the efforts to recover were going to be just as emotionally heavy. The emotional scales need to be balanced (you can't be angry or sad forever), so prepare yourself when getting help, because there are people out there that care about you and want you to be better. Once you are healthy, you can go back to the bridges you no doubt burned down before realizing your injury, those with family and loved ones. Repairing those relationships is also part of the recovery.

One of the methods I've used to handle flareups, which in the past, have normally sent me down a road of self-medicating through either alcoholism, binge eating, or another coping mechanism, are breathing techniques. While training in close-quarter battle scenarios, when the 'stack' of operators is preparing to breach through a door, the last man in the stack is instructed to take a breath, let it out and 'squeeze' (reaching out and squeezing the leg or the tricep of the person in front of them), the next operator in the stack. That lets the operator know that the person behind them is ready to go, and now, in turn, that individual also takes a breath and 'squeezes' up the line. This happens until the operator closest to the door gets the last 'squeeze', then after his tactical breath, he readies himself and initiates the breach for the stack. That breathing technique is designed to calm and focus the minds of the operators who are about to engage in a dynamic action. I've used it countless times as a professional, both as a soldier and a police officer, and I learned to use it to calm my mind and focus myself.

I write the final paragraph of this chapter as a message to military and police instructors who are training those who suffer from training scars. When an individual you are teaching has a perceived Training

Post-Traumatic Growth

Scar, your workload doubles. You have a duty to help that person unlearn the older, conflicting, skillset that is counterintuitive to the currently superior one. There will be relapses occasionally, and that's to be expected because the person has utilized the previous skill thousands of times, with success. It takes time and repetition to unlearn the old skill in place of the new one being taught. It is time consuming, and it takes longer to 'retrain' someone who has Training Scars than it does to teach a person who has zero experience in the subject matter. It's important for both the instructor and the individual to remove their ego from the equation. Once the new foundation is laid out, take the individual aside to practice repetition in a safe environment that won't cause anxiety. It almost sounds like I'm asking you to baby these people who have such specialized and honed skillsets, but sometimes the previously learned skills are so hard to unlearn that you need to break it down to the basics and take the time required to address the psychological and neurological side of the skill, and its history, with the individual. Only then can they hone their actions into the lessons being taught to them.

Chapter 11
Equine Therapy

I met my wife in February of 2020. We met in a small pub, and I had no idea what to expect. She was the first date I'd had since leaving my ex-wife, and I had two young children I was responsible for. We sat there for hours until the live band was done playing, and I learned about how she had grown up with horses, competed professionally throughout her whole life, as well as trained horses of all backgrounds and taught others both horsemanship and horseback riding. She has helped me recover from the injuries I suffered from. She has her own personal experience with the trauma of mental health injuries – her uncle was diagnosed with PTSD as a former RCMP officer. She was one of the last people to see him alive, as he tragically lost his life to the injury. One of the therapeutic methods I used, but didn't expect or think of as a method of treatment, and was therefore engaged in without the purpose of therapeutic benefits, was Equine Therapy, otherwise known as 'horse therapy'.

I had never heard of Equine Therapy before meeting my wife. After going through it with her, I stand by it 100%. Rehabilitation in veterans who suffer from mental health injuries can be complicated, and in my case, it led to moments where I would overreact, become irrationally angry at an insignificant slight, or simply be too anxious and reactive to stimulus I was presented with in the moment. I know several first responders, generally veterans from the military, who were hesitant to seek out help for fear of being labeled as 'weak'. I was initially hesitant to speak with someone, not only because of the stigma of a soldier seeking mental health assistance, but also because I didn't think I'd find anyone that could understand what I had gone through. As first responders, each traumatic situation is unique and has its own hurdles to overcome. In my case, I had concerns that I wouldn't be able to get a civilian to understand what I had experienced without perhaps thinking that either: I'm a monster for how I reacted in those situations or, they'd be clueless as to how to approach such trauma. I eventually recognized and acknowledged that my assumptions were incorrect stereotypes and I proactively sought help. I went through several different therapists and therapeutic methods until I found one that fit. He was a former police officer himself and had his own personal trauma that he had worked through in the past. That familiarity and understanding between us helped foster a rapport which provided me the comfort I needed to talk about what was bothering me most. It took years for me to find someone that I could feel comfortable talking to, and I know for some people it can feel near impossible to find that level of comfort with another human being. That being said, I've found a way to seek therapy without having to talk or worry about being judged, and that's through working with horses.

Equine Therapy is not an excuse to avoid people, but rather another avenue to seek treatment. It's important to not become a recluse and practice avoidance behaviour, as I've written about in previous chapters. The unique benefit of Equine Therapy is that it can be used as a mirror of a person's behaviour and mannerisms. Animals, especially empathetic ones such as horses, are adept at reading the body language of a person, and react appropriately. Much like injured veterans and first responders who are in a hypervigilant state of "Fight or Flight" response, horses, as prey animals, can be just as jumpy, especially in certain circumstances.

Equine therapy as a pathway, also referred to as Equine Assisted Learning (EAL) or Equine Facilitated Learning (EFL), has been used to assist with more than veterans and first responders. Other members of society such as those with autism, domestic abuse survivors, individuals in addictions treatment, leadership skills training, and those suffering from symptoms of grief and loss can all benefit from equine therapy. Equine Facilitated Psychotherapy (a qualification I will have completed by the time this book is published), and Equine Facilitated Learning, are certifications offered by Dr. Veronica Lac and the HERD Institute. These equine therapy models have been used to work with high-risk teens, victims of domestic abuse, spouses of veterans, first responders, children with eating disorders, and persons with anxiety, depression, and addiction issues. The formal training for prospective Equine Therapists is provided by companies with trained Equine Assisted Learning instructors, such as Equine Assisted Growth and Learning Association (EAGALA) Therapists or the HERD Institute, among others. Sessions are overseen by a psychologist or psychotherapist, and the EAL Facilitator helps bond the client to a horse; just like picking a mental health professional, it will take a special connection for the pairing to work. With Equine Therapy however, the client doesn't always pick the professional, rather the horse can pick the client. The relationship between horse and client cannot be forced, and surrendering yourself to the concept that no matter how hard you want something to succeed, if the equine doesn't fit with you, then the therapy will not take. Studies have proven that within twenty minutes of exposure to equines, the stress hormone cortisol reduces in the humans involved. (Malinowski et al., 2018)

When I was first introduced to horses it was informal. Honestly, I was just joining my wife at the barn and wanted to partake in riding with her, so she began to show me the ropes. I didn't complete any official or developed programs, nor get registered in a class to help veterans or first responders become acquainted in a therapeutic equine program. No, I got hooked into a relationship with a cowgirl who has a passion and history for horses like I've never seen before. She lives on a twenty-five-acre farm, much of it either forested or sectioned into large horse paddocks. She owned six horses when I first met her, used primarily at the time for different equine sports. One of them is nearly entirely blind, her name is Isabelle. She had suffered from what is believed to be a genetic issue and was injured, causing her sight to fade to blindness over the years. It was tragic for both the horse and my wife, as she had aspirations to compete in the Olympics with Isabelle. She had to spend a year retraining Isabelle to listen, ride, and work with confidence all over again. Isabelle recovered so well that when I first met the herd, I couldn't determine that she was blind at all. Other than a slight cocking of her head to the side, and her ears moving to listen to any, and all, noise around her, she appeared and acted just like any other horse I'd never have known, not that I had known many!

Each horse has its own personality, some being haughty and flighty and others being immensely curious and bold. Each of them, regardless of personality, had a calming effect on me and were welcoming of a new human being exposed to them. I had met horses before, but for short spurts of time for quick pats. I hadn't spent any significant time with them, nor had I done any work with equines before. These two-thousand-pound animals were large and powerful, capable of killing me with a single kick, but at the same time were fragile, gentle, and required constant attention and care.

I quickly realized how intelligent they were. Once I began spending more time with them, I saw how empathetic they are with humans. My first experience in the Equine Therapy world, without knowing it would be Equine Therapy, was simply being introduced to the herd. I saw them through a fence and my wife decided to bring in Isabelle to the barn and properly introduce her to me. Once inside, my wife taught me how to interact and introduce myself to her, lifting my hand out so she could sniff me. It wasn't shortly after that I realized that I 'clicked' with Isabelle, the blind mare. My wife helped me, and she took out a grooming kit and taught me how to brush her. I was taught the basic forms of care on a horse including how to walk her with a lead rope (like a dog leash but for horse). The more I went through the motions caring for the horse, the more my wife encouraged me to talk to Isabelle and be in the moment with her. Because Isabelle is blind, talking to her lets her know where you are while working around her body in the barn. Communicating with her ensured I didn't 'spook' (startle) her by accident. It seemed silly to me at the time, speaking comforting and encouraging words to an animal that weighed a couple thousand pounds and was much taller than me. It worked though, and I could see the relaxation take hold as I worked and talked with her. I realized, after that hour I had worked with her before taking her back to the paddock, my anxiety and anger had subsided. I was calm and happy, and then I talked to my wife about the entire experience and she answered questions I had the entire time.

I continued working with Isabelle for months after that, interacting with her constantly and learning how to handle her. If my wife needed to work on her for something I hadn't had the opportunity to learn yet, whether it was hoof-care or something else, Isabelle would rest her head on my shoulder and start to fall asleep standing up. Her head was so heavy I'd have to brace myself in preparation for her to go limp on me, otherwise that giant head, weighing over sixty pounds, would have pushed me over. We quickly learned about one another, with her recognizing my voice from across the paddock when I called out and with me recognizing how she was feeling and what she wanted while I was working on grooming her. Once I had spent considerable time working on the basics, my wife showed me how to 'tack up' a horse, known to laymen such as me, as putting on her saddle, bridle, and other equipment so we could get riding.

My self-esteem with Isabelle up to this point had hit a high, and the comfort level and connection we had together eliminated any nervousness of me learning to ride her. I was taught how to mount and dismount her gently, and how to hold the reins. Everything went well at first, and I learned that the pressure of my legs on her body would be what dictated whether she picked up the pace or not, and individual pressure on either side would cause her to move her body left and right. I could also use the reins to help turn and halt her when needed. Everything went well as I was taught the basics of walking, but my stress increased once I started to learn how to move faster. I have a hip injury due to my time served in the army, and I'll eventually need a hip replacement. This had led to a lack of flexibility in my hip which makes it difficult to ride sometimes, or do anything else more dynamic. I began struggling with the lessons of trotting and cantering, and I was getting frustrated with myself. Isabelle took notice of my change in temperament, and although I wasn't being hard on her, she mirrored my attitude and she began getting frustrated as well. This compounding negativity that we were both experiencing made one particular ride less-than-fun and my wife noticed as well, encouraging a break. I stopped early to walk her around and it was at that moment that my wife helped me realize that she was simply mirroring my emotions right back at me. She wasn't doing anything wrong, and the more worked up I got, the worse she reacted. After I got off, my wife hopped on her and I recognized immediately that the horse relaxed and started reacting to the positive mannerisms that my wife was giving her. It was eye-opening for me. She is the type of horse someone needs to work *with*, not command and expect blind obedience (most are that way, actually!). This realization made me take a step back both mentally and physically, and I saw that once I did, I calmed down and Isabelle responded in kind. I'm thankful she didn't hold it against me, and we work together to this day. That experience was eye-opening for me, with the instruction I received on top of the interaction with Isabelle opening up my ability to communicate, trust, and regulate my emotions with her. It reduced my feelings of isolation and it enabled me to build a sense of connection with her. It was shortly thereafter I was able to ride her alone and now we're the best-of-friends.

Interaction with such large, empathetic animals I do not feel can be explained well enough in words and should be experienced in person. In my experience, informal Equine Therapy taught me to be a good listener and interpreter of non-verbal communications. I've learned how my emotional reactions, whether they are positive or negative, impact those around me. I've also learned how trust works both ways, and how teamwork was the only way I was going to get through a day's work during the therapy. I learned that it's impossible to lie to a horse, and that no matter what kind of face I put on when walking into a session with a horse, they can sense through my body language and mannerisms whether or not I'm having a good day. Fun Fact: Horses can hear a human heartbeat from 4 feet away and interpret it; they also sense energetic shifts and facial expressions as well as body language and moods (McComb, K., Young, J. J. R., et al. (2016).

Finally, after taking into account all of the psychological benefits of Equine Therapy, one of the best parts for me was feeling the physical exhaustion of a hard day of working outside. Whether it was grooming, hauling hay, riding for hours, or putting up and installing fences for paddocks, I left each day feeling that familiar physical workout completed. Caring for them was satisfying in and of itself, as it provided me purpose and I could tell they were grateful. Over time, Isabelle and the other horses began approaching me of their own accord, seeking my attention by nudging me, allowing me to touch them, and trusting me to lead them around when necessary. I was quickly becoming their friend. That was important to me. Years of leaving traditional therapy/counselling sessions mentally exhausted and raw but physically agitated, even jittery afterwards, was tough. This change was refreshing and fulfilling. With Equine Therapy, I physically felt that I accomplished something, and completed a mental health exercise at the same time, even though the primary objective was caring for the horse. I've never had that before, and it is an excellent experience. I recommend Equine Therapy to anyone who has access to it. I can honestly say it's changed my life for the better, and granted me positive memories that I can reflect upon. I was able to establish a friendship and bond with another living creature without fear of judgement or criticism, something I didn't think was possible at the time. A safe environment like that is absolutely necessary in order to gain perspective about oneself and to heal openly. Though no one is ever quite done learning, I've accomplished a lot and continue to grow each day – especially days I'm with the herd.

On a personal note, this experience changed me in such a positive way that my wife and I worked to dedicate ourselves to helping other veterans through equine therapy methods. We have both since received

Post-Traumatic Growth

certification in the field and opened our own business 'Equine Endeavours Therapy' just outside of Ottawa, Ontario. It is our mission to help first responders recover from trauma without the expectation of having to talk to another human. Being present in the moment with an equine partner and talking to them can be rewarding and therapeutic in-and-of itself.

Chapter 12
Post-Traumatic Growth

Throughout this book, I've gone through several different scenarios where I've experienced psychological issues both during, and long after, the traumatic event occurred. The psychological injuries that affected my mental health and the combination of symptoms culminated to a diagnosis of Post Traumatic Stress Disorder. I learned that simply having resilience is usually enough to solidify myself against the symptoms of the injury. Humans are built for resiliency, and we tend to find renewed strength and fortitude in times of crisis. Humans experiencing traumatic events is not uncommon, and the majority of people have reported having gone through at least one traumatic event in their lifetime (Bremner et al., 2006). This could be the death of a parent or loved one, exposure to a car accident, being a victim of a violent crime, or any other experience they feel traumatizing. It seems near impossible to avoid experiencing tragedy in one form or another over a lifetime. Resilience in relation to PTSD is what allows a person suffering from a PTSI to eventually bounce back to the way they were prior to the injury. The difference between Post-Traumatic Resiliency and Post-Traumatic Growth (PTG) is that the individual *grows* from the trauma, instead of bouncing back to the way they were before. I first learned about PTG by accident, by talking about how healthy I

Post-Traumatic Growth

was to my psychologist. They helped explain to me that what I was going through and feeling after all the therapy was basically becoming a better person. I knew at the time I was healthier, but I didn't know there was a name for coming out positive on the other side of psychological injuries. I am thrilled that it's common enough for those feelings of personal strength, improved relationships and changes in priorities to have a designated name.

Post-Traumatic Growth takes many forms after the healing process, and as the symptoms of the injury begin to subside with treatment, the growth starts to begin. Post-Traumatic Growth cannot be attained solely through the efforts of recovery, but also through perspective. Exposure to support groups can help speed up the ability to gain a degree of growth by exposing yourself to those who have already experienced it, as it was in my case. Peer support groups led by others who have suffered a PTSI are good candidates to provide the wisdom of Post-Traumatic Growth, but only if the person receiving these lessons is open to changing their perspective; growth is impossible to achieve if the person perceives the injury as ongoing, without efforts to alleviate symptoms. Post-Traumatic Growth can only take place once the healing is complete and the walls of resiliency and self-preservation lower to a point where we can allow our minds to be consciously vulnerable to new perspectives.

Post-Traumatic Growth can be many things. The experience of trauma can lead people to a greater sense of self-awareness, resilience, and confidence in their ability to overcome adversity. It causes people to re-evaluate their priorities and values, putting the important aspects of their life into perspective. It is possible that it leads to deeper relationships with others, appreciation of deeper spiritual values, optimism for every new day, a grander perspective and thankfulness of life's priorities, and a stronger sense of self and capabilities/capacity to handle future difficulties that life may throw our way (Tedeschi, R. G., & Calhoun, 2004). To boil it down to its roots, PTG is the ability to gain a new and greater appreciation for life post-trauma. The trauma does not have to be related to a diagnosis of PTSD. It can be a survivor of cancer who has gone through extensive surgery or chemotherapy and come out the other side with a new perspective on life. Trauma, outside of the negative impacts it has, allows a person to learn, understand, and appreciate the new perspectives and attitudes that result from a traumatic experience. It's an opportunity for growth after healing.

The concept of Post-Traumatic Growth was created by Richard Tedeshi and Lawrence Calhoun of the University of North Carolina in the mid 1990's (Tedeschi, R. G., & Calhoun, 2004). They have written extensively on how people who experience psychological struggles following traumatic events can see positive personal growth afterwards (Tedeschi, R. G., & Calhoun, 2004). Tedeshi and Calhoun specifically mentioned cancer survivors, survivors of plane crashes and individuals that served in the Vietnam war. For people suffering from the psychological after-effects of trauma, being told to look at the potential to have a positive transformational effect is a hard pill to swallow; although history has shown that positive transformational growth is not only possible, but rooted into many cultures and religions as part of how a person can grow. In Christianity for example, the crucifixion and death of Jesus is a major theme in the bible, and the suffering Jesus experienced had a direct transformative effect on every man and woman on earth.

I won't continue to bore you with statistics, but it's important to me to show the clear evidence that what I've experienced personally with Post-Traumatic Growth can be replicated and manifested in others, and is common for people who have survived PTSD. I find it difficult to stomach when I hear people speak about PTSD as if it's a chronic and permanent injury. I've seen people become victimized by their symptoms and allow the issue to become a permanent part of their character – it becomes how they identify themselves and with others around them. I was exposed to this prior to any psychological injury from either the military or my previous policing career. This example was in my uncle, who served in the military through the 1980's and 1990's. He was exposed to several horrors, including events while on a United Nations (UN) mission to Rwanda, where he was forced to witness, and not intervene, in the genocide that occurred in 1994. It was estimated that up to, and over, one million men, women and children were slaughtered. Deaths were by machete and it was common to see children with missing limbs as a message sent from rival Hutu to the slaughtered Tutsi's. There were wells filled with the bodies of the dead left to rot, and as members of the UN mission, they had strict rules of engagement (ROE's) that practically hamstrung them from legally intervening in the genocide with any effectiveness. They could prevent nothing.

My uncle returned from that UN mission and he was never the same. Support within the military ranks at that time with regards to mental health was not widely supported and still in its infancy. Mental health support and resources for soldiers and other first responder style careers was met with raised eyebrows, and to this day, there remains a degree of taboo for people who were 'not mentally fit enough' or who were 'weak minded' when it comes to psychological injuries. Because those resources were not immediately available, my uncle didn't realize the extent of his injury, and like many others, it would be years before he was able to get the help he required. The delay in help caused more issues, and although he is much better than before, he suffers sporadically from symptoms related to the injury. He remains aware of his injuries and removes himself from situations where he may be triggered into an episode of anxiety, panic, anger, or any other extreme emotion. He has prescribed medication that allows him to handle specific issues, and they also allow him to sleep at night, otherwise his mind refuses to calm to a point of relaxation.

Men like my uncle, my cousin, my close friends who are first responders (Fire Fighters, Police Officers, Paramedics) and myself, all define ourselves to a certain degree by our careers. Certain careers attract people because of what the career represents. Doctors, police officers, firefighters, nurses, and paramedics are all careers that supposedly represent a higher morality. They are jobs that help people, or serve their city or country. Because these professions are presented to the public as 'noble' in nature, it's not uncommon for those who work them to define themselves through their work. These careers demand so much of the person, as well as their loved ones, both emotionally and physically, that it's no surprise that our character is defined by them. Western culture romanticizes these careers to the point of hero-worship, making others believe there is a moral high ground associated with these types of careers. That romanticization and the concept of "Service Before Self" can create generations of first responders who take after their parents or grandparents, much as it did for me. I think it's natural that we, as humans, define ourselves by our actions. Especially in the career of a first responder, where our actions are routinely linked with life-altering circumstances in the situations that are responded to.

What I have seen however, and what prevents Post-Traumatic Growth from occurring, is allowing our psychological injuries, or what others call PTSD or PTSIs, define us, instead of our actions. When I was suffering from my PTSI, something insignificant would make me irrationally angry and I would end up stewing on that anger for days at a time.

Post-Traumatic Growth

Personal Anecdote
Dealing with Anger

One day in particular happened in 2018. My son was walking and my daughter had just been born. We decided to go to the museum of civilization, with my ex-wife caring for my daughter who was breastfeeding. My son to this day absolutely adores escalators, and if I take him to the mall he will ask, if not outright demand, that we go on every escalator we walk past. There was an escalator in the museum that went from the main level down into the lower floor that held the second half of the museum and the cafeteria. The museum was very slow that day, and no one was attempting to ride the escalator up or down to the different levels except my son and I. There was an employee at the top of the escalator checking our tickets before descending, and my son waved to him as we descended. He, at two years old, asked if he could go up the escalator again and the two of us held hands and went back up the escalator, with him grinning like a madman the entire time, looking around and staring up at me. He was the happiest kid in the world in those moments.

We went down the escalator and back up twice, still the only ones on it. My son wasn't 'horsing around', and had been holding my hand the entire time. Once we ascended the second time, the employee at the top of the escalator checking tickets stopped me and told me I couldn't abuse the escalator and play on it any longer. I instantly had anger flow over me to the point that I could barely contain it. I knew that my son and I weren't playing on the escalator, and someone policing my one-on-one time with my son must have had a death wish. I didn't want to upset my son however, and I told the man I wouldn't go on it any more. In my head though, I had already planned on throwing him over the railing fifteen feet below, onto the concrete floor. I had to consciously stop myself from escalating the situation and my mood was ruined for days afterwards. I knew that I was irrationally angry, but I couldn't shake the mood or feeling. I was near homicidal and wanted to kill that man for having the audacity to interrupt my father-son time. It took several days for my mood to come back to normal and I was moody and irritable the entire time, to everyone around me. I knew enough about myself, even then, that I could reason the 'why' I was angry, but I couldn't shake the feeling for an extended period of time. That entire time I was stewing inside, imagining the ways I wanted to kill that person. It consumed me, and my mood suffered for it. After several days, I was able to shake that angry weight off my soul and move on.

Post-Traumatic Growth

Such an insignificant incident as an escalator ride with my son being shortened by a museum employee should never have had the extreme effect on me that it did. My anger and impatience had come to a point where nobody could negotiate with me about my mood anymore. I would, and could, acknowledge with people around me that I was angry and that I couldn't calm down in the moment, and needed extended time to myself. After I initiated the Cognitive Behavioural Therapy with my psychologist, as well as utilizing meditation techniques, I began making progress over the more serious PTSI symptoms and that allowed me to deal with my anger issues at the same time.

During those long months however, I had fallen into a slippery slope of blaming some of my issues on the diagnosis I had received. It was easy to look at a diagnosis and blame symptoms related to it on the paperwork I had received confirming the issue. I recognized however, that by blaming the symptoms of the PTSI on the diagnosis, that the reality was that I was avoiding taking responsibility for my own actions. At the end of the day, I was preventing myself from taking responsibility for my own reactions to the stimuli around me, and by doing so, I was preventing myself from recovering from the injury and having any amount of Post-Traumatic Growth. One of the lessons I learned that helped me address my PTSIs and engage in the therapy needed to get to a point where I gained a new appreciation in life, was from a mentor of mine who explained the concept of the "Man in the Mirror".

A former Staff Sergeant with the police, and now an Inspector within the same service, he worked opposite shifts as me. I would routinely see him at the front desk monitoring situations and directing officers on priority calls when necessary. He is a leader and an experienced man in personal trauma, having lost his own adult son to cancer only a few years earlier. He is passionate about policing and cares deeply for the well-being of all officers working the front line. He is cognizant of mental health trauma that effects the front lines of policing and is not shy when talking about how we, as a whole, need to be more empathetic to those in need of help. In summary, he is a caring man who is wise beyond his years. He and I would talk sometimes before and after shift when I saw him, and he recognized that I was suffering at the time. He explained to me a technique taught to him many years earlier which helped him realize he wasn't living up to his potential as well. He told me that every day I needed to look myself in the mirror at the beginning and end of each day. I needed to take a look at my reflection and ask myself what I was going to do to become a better person for myself and my children. At the end of the day, I needed to look again and ask myself if what I did that day bettered me and the people I interacted with. I started doing that every day and I found it helped temper my reactions to stimulus because at the end of the day, after everything had calmed down, I had to look at myself and take responsibility for my actions in the mirror. I couldn't shy away from that anymore and no matter what the diagnosis I had at the time was, I was still going to look at the same man in the mirror twice a day and I had to come to terms with myself.

That lesson, combined with the counselling, Cognitive Behavioural Therapy, and time to come to terms with myself, helped me gain new perspective. I grew out of my injury, being aware that, similar to an injured ligament or tendon, I would need to be aware of the previous injury going forward to ensure that I wouldn't "re-injure" myself again. This self-awareness allowed me realize that the injury doesn't define who I am as a person, rather I define myself by how I overcome that injury and make myself better for it. Having a PTSI is an extremely humbling injury to go through, it breaks a person down to a level where the only thing they feel is the injury itself. It can become very easy to allow the injury to define us, largely in part due to the constant presence it has in every facet of our lives. The injury is invisible to everyone but the person it affects. It's likely that they have suffered for a significant period of time before realizing the extent of the injury and getting the help needed to eliminate the symptoms. Although resources to get help with PTSI symptoms are more widely available than ever, including peer support groups that have members who have also suffered from psychological injuries, the only person capable and responsible for fixing you is YOU. Steps must be taken with your own two feet, and although there are resources available to help make those

Post-Traumatic Growth

steps easier, the momentum to begin the path to healing is the responsibility of the person who has the injury.

I can tell you though, because the statistics now exist, and I can personally attest to it: it gets better. You will recover and you will gain a new appreciation for life. You'll find joy in things that you took for granted before the injury, as well as joy in being able to experience new interactions and situations in life instead of resenting them or hiding from them. I grew to appreciate new life dreams and goals that I didn't previously have. I learned not to define myself by my career or my injuries, but through my actions as a man. I believe my personality has changed to a more grounded, well-rounded person who makes efforts to process situations. This allows me to wait, and not jump to conclusions or overreact, to stimulus any longer. The recovery process tempered my ego, and I have a new respect for the invisible injuries that I assume many people around me deal with at a personal level every day. I tackled the negative stimulus, dealt with, and respected it, and then used that experience to become better from it. It was a hard life lesson to go through, and took time. Many others have, and will, go through similar processes in the future. Whether a cancer survivor, PTSD survivor, or any other survivor of a traumatic experience, it's possible to have a higher self-worth and well-being after recovery.

The wisdom gained from going through trauma, recovery, and coming out of such hardship cannot be overstated. Those circumstances define you going forward, and ultimately, how you are defined is a decision you need to make. The road going forward is full of pain, stumbles into short relapses and heartache, but it's possible to get through it. You may not be the same person you were prior to the trauma, but so long as you keep working on yourself, you'll be better than before, and love and appreciate the person that you've become.

At least, that's what happened for me.

I'm better because I experienced that pain and came out the other side. After years of counselling and hard work, with loved ones and peers to help when needed, I came out stronger. I'm not the same person I was before the injury. I'm a better one. A stronger one.

References

Abbot, C., Barber, E., Burke, B., Harvey, J., Newland, C., Rose, M., & Young, A. (2015). What's killing our medics? Ambulance Service Manager Program. Conifer, CO: Reviving Responders. Retrieved from http://www. revivingresponders.com/originalpaper

Bremner, J. D., Vermetten, E., Soufer, R., & Staib, L. H. (2006). The impact of cumulative trauma on mental health. Journal of Clinical Psychiatry, 67(1), 18–22. https://doi.org/10.4088/JCP.v67n0104

National Counterterrorism Center (NCTC). (n.d.). Ansar al-Sharia. [Website]. Retrieved February 6, 2023, from https://www.dni.gov/nctc/groups/ansar_al_sharia.html.

Dorahy, M. J., & Van der Hart, O. (2014). Trauma-focused integrative treatment for individuals with dissociative identity disorder and complex posttraumatic stress disorder. Onno van der Hart, 49-70.

National Institute of Mental Health (NIMH). (2021). Post-traumatic stress disorder (PTSD). Retrieved from https://www.nimh.nih.gov/health/topics/post-traumatic-stress-disorder-ptsd/index.shtml

https://www.onnovdhart.nl/articles/DorarhyVanderHart2014.pdf (Pg 11 of 22) (Putnam et al., 1996)

M.B. Powers et al. www.sciencedirect.com/science/article/abs/pii/S027273581000070X Clinical Psychology Review (2010)

A. Van Minnen et al. https://www.sciencedirect.com/science/article/abs/pii/S0005796701000249 Behaviour Research and Therapy (2002)

J. Cukor et al. Evidence-based treatments for PTSD, new directions, and special challenges Psychiatric and Neurologic Aspects of War (2010)

Hyman, R. (1953). Stimulus information as a determinant of reaction time. Journal of Experimental Psychology, 46(2), 188-196.

Kornblum, S., Hasbroucq, T., & Osman, A. (1990). Dimensional Overlap: Cognitive Basis for Stimulus-Response Compatibility—A Model and Taxonomy. University of Michigan. Cognitive Neurosciences Unit, Centre National de la Recherche Scientifique, Marseille, France, University of California, San Diego. https://www.ncbi.nlm.nih.gov/pmc/articles/PMC2366105

Apfel, B. A., Ross, J., Hlavin, J., Meyerhoff, D. J., Metzler, T. J., Marmar, C. R., Weiner, M. W., Schuff, N., & Neylan, T. C. (2011). Hippocampal volume differences in Gulf War veterans with current versus lifetime posttraumatic stress disorder symptoms. Biological psychiatry, 69(6), 541–548. https://doi.org/10.1016/j.biopsych.2010.09.044

https://www.researchgate.net/publication/15707358_Posttraumatic_Stress_Disorder_in_the_National_Comorbidity_Survey

Cherry KE. Traumatic Stress and Long-Term Recovery: Coping with Disasters and Other Negative Life Events. Springer International Publishing; 2015.

References

Tedeschi, R. G., & Calhoun, L. G. (2004). Posttraumatic growth: Conceptual foundations and empirical evidence. Psychological Inquiry, 15(1), 1-18. doi: 10.1207/s15327965-pli1501_01
https://www.sciencedirect.com/science/article/pii/S0737080617307761
https://web.archive.org/web/20090704085156/http://www.lib.utexas.edu/etd/d/2005/duntleyj48072/duntleyj48072.pdf

VanDenKerkhof EG, Macdonald HM, Jones GT, Power C, Macfarlane GJ. Diet, lifestyle and chronic widespread pain: results from the 1958 British Birth Cohort Study. Pain Res Manag 2011; 16:87–92.

Stanley, I. H., Hom, M. A., Hagan, C. R., & Joiner, T. E. (2015). Career prevalence and correlates of suicidal thoughts and behaviors among firefighters. Journal of Affective Disorders, 187, 163–171. http://dx.doi.org/10.1016/j.jad.2015.08.007

Haddock, C. K., Poston, W. S. C., Jahnke, S. A., & Jitnarin, N. (2017). Alcohol use and problem drinking among women firefighters. Women's Health Issues, 27(6), 632–638. https://doi.org/10.1016/j.whi.2017.07.003

Grossman D. & Christensen L. W. (2008). On combat : the psychology and physiology of deadly conflict in war and in peace (3rd ed.). Warrior Science Pub.

Blais, R. K., Cruz, R. A., Hoyt, T., & Monteith, L. L. (2023). Stigma for seeking psychological help for military sexual trauma is associated with more frequent suicidal ideation among women service members and veterans. Psychology of Violence. https://doi.org/10.1037/vio0000461

Malinowski, K., Yee, C., Tevlin, J. M., Birks, E. K., Durando, M. M., Pournajafi-Nazarloo, H., Cavaiola, A. A., & McKeever, K. H. (2018). The Effects of Equine Assisted Therapy on Plasma Cortisol and Oxytocin Concentrations and Heart Rate Variability in Horses and Measures of Symptoms of Post-Traumatic Stress Disorder in Veterans. Journal of Equine Veterinary Science, 64, 17-26. https://doi.org/10.1016/j.jevs.2018.01.011

Maynard, C., Trivedi, R., Nelson, K., & Fihn, S. D. (2018). Disability Rating, Age at Death, and Cause of Death in U.S. Veterans with Service-Connected Conditions. Military medicine, 183(11-12), e371–e376. https://doi.org/10.1093/milmed/usy040

Kenrick, D. T., & Sheets, V. (1993). Homicidal fantasies. Ethology and Sociobiology, 14(4), 231-246. https://doi.org/10.1016/0162-3095(93)90019-E.

Ryder, M., & Downs, C. (2022). Rethinking reflective practice: John Boyd's OODA loop as an alternative to Kolb. The International Journal of Management Education, 20(3). https://doi.org/10.1016/j.ijme.2022.100703

Wagner, A. C., Torbit, L., Jenzer, T., Landy, M. S., Pukay-Martin, N. D., Macdonald, A., Fredman, S. J., & Monson, C. M. (2016). The Role of Posttraumatic Growth in a Randomized Controlled Trial of Cognitive-Behavioral Conjoint Therapy for PTSD. Journal of traumatic stress, 29(4), 379–383. https://doi.org/10.1002/jts.22122

Proctor, R. W., & Schneider, D. W. (2004). Hicks' law for choice reaction time: A review. Acta Psychologica, 118(3), 229-242.

Hick, W.E. (1952). "On the rate of gain of information" (PDF). Quarterly Journal of Experimental Psychology. 4 (4:1): 11–26. doi:10.1080/17470215208416600.

References

Richards, C. (2012, March 21). Boyd's OODA Loop (It's Not What You Think). J. Addams & Partners, Inc. crichards@jaddams.com.

Smith, M. E. (2005). Bilateral hippocampal volume reduction in adults with post-traumatic stress disorder: A meta-analysis of structural MRI studies. Hippocampus, 15(6), 767-771. https://doi.org/10.1002/hipo.20102

Samuelson K. W. (2011). Post-traumatic stress disorder and declarative memory functioning: a review. Dialogues in clinical neuroscience, 13(3), 346–351. https://doi.org/10.31887/DCNS.2011.13.2/ksamuelson

www.ingramcontent.com/pod-product-compliance
Lightning Source LLC
Chambersburg PA
CBHW061738070526
44585CB00024B/2719